MEN-AT-ARMS SERIES
EDITOR: PHILIP WARNER

The Coldstream Guards

Text by CHARLES GRANT

Colour plates by MICHAEL ROFFE

OSPREY PUBLISHING LIMITED

Published in England by
Osprey Publishing Ltd,
P.O. Box 25, 707 Oxford Road, Reading, Berkshire
© Copyright 1971 Osprey Publishing Ltd

SBN 85045 057 8

The author and publishers would like to thank The Guards Museum for their kind assistance with the illustrations.

Printed in Great Britain by
Jarrold & Sons Ltd, Norwich

Monck's Regiment

Of all places which have given their names to fighting units, there can be fewer of less importance than the village of Coldstream. Situated on the Scottish side of the River Tweed, which forms the ancient border between Scotland and England, the name of this little village is part of the title of Her Majesty's 2nd Regiment of Foot Guards, which has distinguished itself in some of the greatest battles in Britain's history.

To find the reason why the 2nd Foot Guards should be called the Coldstream Guards, we have to seek back to the later years of the English Civil War. In June of 1650, Cromwell the Lord Protector wished to create a regiment of foot to be commanded by George Monck, a fine soldier who had originally fought on the Royalist side but was now a staunch Parliamentarian. It seems that the first regiment to which Monck was tentatively appointed was not too enthusiastic about having an ex-Royalist colonel, and the problem was consequently solved by the creation of an entirely new unit. Five companies were taken from each of the foot regiments of Sir Arthur Hazelrigg and George Fenwick, stationed at the time – that is, just before Cromwell's advance into Scotland – at Newcastle and Berwick respectively, and amalgamated into one unit. In due course these companies joined up and marched northwards in the army of Cromwell as Monck's Regiment of Foot.

In July 1650 the Parliamentarian army passed through Berwickshire and Edinburgh, and with Monck's regiment well to the fore, met the Scots at Dunbar. The battle was a complete victory for Cromwell. In the battle Monck distinguished himself by advancing half-pike in hand at the head of his regiment. According to later correspondence of Cromwell himself he had much to

Gen. George Monck, Duke of Albemarle, first Colonel of the Coldstream Guards – then called Monck's Regiment – 1650–70 (National Portrait Gallery)

do with the direction of operations which defeated the Scots in 'less than half an hour's dispute'.

There was still much to be done, for numerous garrisons in various strong places were holding out dourly against the forces of the English Parliament. Monck, who had been promoted to general's rank, was busily occupied in reducing the garrisons of these fortresses. He besieged Edinburgh Castle which, despite its reputation for impregnability, capitulated; as did Tantallon Castle the following year, famous in Sir Walter Scott's *Marmion*. On all occasions Monck's Regiment of Foot was with him, and he was in the act of laying siege to Stirling Castle when the resuscitated Scots army marched southwards into England on the invasion which was to end in their defeat by Cromwell at Worcester. After this battle – a near death-blow to the Stuarts – Monck carried on with the business of pacification, and accepted the surrender of Stirling Castle. He then marched to Dundee, which he seized, followed in quick succession by the taking of Montrose, Aberdeen and Dunbarton. Then, enjoying the considerable status of Commissioner for Scots Affairs, Monck returned to London in 1652, leaving his regiment in Scotland. During the time he was away from Scotland he served with some distinction at sea, but he was back in the north when the Lord Protector died in 1658. It was as General Commanding in Scotland in fact that he received the news of Cromwell's death, and in that capacity he proclaimed Richard Cromwell as Lord Protector in succession to his father.

However, it became rapidly evident that little of the authority of the first Lord Protector had descended to his son. Discontent was rife, and in October 1659 Monck found it necessary to address the officers of his regiment in Edinburgh, making it clear that he was for constitutionally appointed authority and against the use of military force to influence Parliament, as it seemed was threatened in London. But events were moving rapidly towards the point where some decision would have to be made if civil stability was to be maintained, and in December he assembled his entire command at the village of Coldstream, where his own

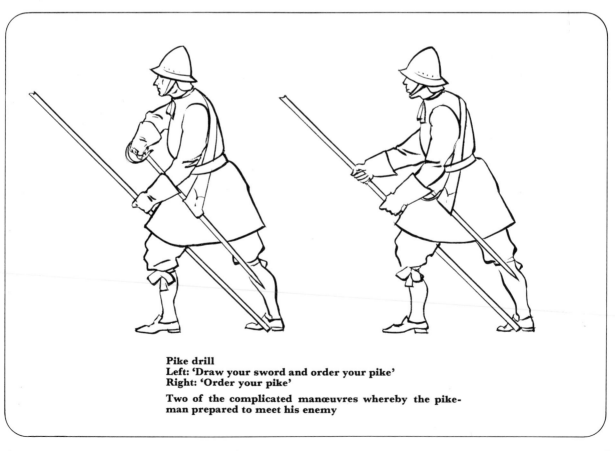

Pike drill
Left: 'Draw your sword and order your pike'
Right: 'Order your pike'

Two of the complicated manœuvres whereby the pikeman prepared to meet his enemy

regiment was already stationed. On New Year's Day, 1660, like Caesar before the Rubicon, Monck made up his mind and marched his men through the little village whose name his regiment would bear for centuries. They crossed the River Tweed, now swollen and straining at its banks with winter rain and snow, then marched south to London. His regiment, leading the little army, must have made a brave sight – uniforms of red and green, and the colours of the companies boldly fluttering over the pikemen's steel 'pots' and the broad-brimmed hats of the musketeers. Durham was passed on 8th January, and three days later Monck's men entered York. To increasing support from the population Monck pressed forward steadily through snow and blizzards, his own regiment always in the van. At St Albans he wrote to London asking for billets to be prepared for his men, and on 3rd February 1660 he entered London and his troops went into quarters at St James's Palace.

Soon the good behaviour of his men and the General's patent sincerity won favour among the previously somewhat suspicious Londoners, who approved when Monck was created Commander-in-Chief of the Army. It is no part of our story to describe the subsequent political manoeuvrings, and it is enough to say that the end of May was signalled by the Restoration of the monarchy, and Gen. Monck was created Duke of Albemarle by the new King, Charles II. Although the New Model army of Cromwellian days had to be disbanded, it was decided that – alone of all the regiments of foot – Monck's should be retained on the establishment. On 14 February 1661 Monck's Regiment was mustered on Tower Hill, and ordered to lay down its arms and to be declared formally disbanded. Immediately this had been done, the order was given to retrieve the weapons and the regiment commanded to take up arms as the Lord General's Regiment of Foot Guards. At this moment the regiment was officially born. Hats were flung high into the air, the drums thundered and echoed across the Thames, and the soldiers roared out 'God Save King Charles the Second'.

The Seventeenth Century

Active service was not long in coming to the new Guards regiments. In the beginning of 1664, 500 men were recruited as marines on board ships of war, and these men – or some of them – fought in an engagement off Harwich against the Dutch. Their commander was the Duke of York, later James II. In the same year a detachment of Coldstreamers formed part of an expedition to North America; and during the ensuing few years parties of the regiment were involved, as marines, in many sea actions of all kinds. In one such encounter off the coast of Denmark, their commander was none other than the Colonel of the Regiment, the Duke of Albemarle – soldier and sailor, too – who, as a result of the rather heavy losses incurred, was castigated for over-boldness. To this censure it appears the veteran returned a fairly dusty answer.

The Coldstreamers were now recognized as the second senior regiment of Foot Guards. The 1st Guards – the Grenadiers that were to be – had not been previously on the official establishment, but took priority as representing the bodyguard about King Charles before his restoration. The uniform of the Coldstreamers remained the same – the musketeers clad in red with green facings, the pikemen in green with red facings. It would not

Musketeer 1669, showing rear view of the bandoleer of cartridges – the 'twelve apostles' as they were known

Each of the twelve cartridge-cases held one charge of gunpowder, and all were suspended from a crossbelt or bandoleer. This could be pulled round over the left shoulder as each case became empty following the firing of the matchlock musket. Also attached to the bandoleer was a bag for carrying musket balls, a flask containing fine priming powder and a spare match. While in the process of firing, the musketeer would usually carry several musket balls in his mouth for speed when recharging the musket

be many years, however, before the rapid improvements in muskets caused the latter type of soldier to disappear from the ranks of the Coldstream Guards and indeed from every other regiment.

In 1670 General Monck, Duke of Albemarle and Colonel of the Coldstream Guards, died at the age of sixty-two. His body lay in state at Somerset House, and was buried with full military honours at Westminster Abbey. His appointment as Lord General was not passed to any lesser man, and the Earl of Craven was made Colonel of the Regiment. It appears that from this time the regiment was officially known as the Coldstream Guards.

For some time detachments of the Coldstreamers continued to serve with the fleet as marines, but in 1678 the regiment was sent to Flanders. During its short stay there – it returned the following year – it was brigaded with the 1st Guards under probably the most distinguished British soldier of all time, John Churchill, then Earl of Marlborough. This was the first occasion that a brigade of Guards took the field. About this time the regiment consisted of twelve companies, each officially numbering 100 men.

In 1680 a composite unit known as the King's Battalion was raised from the Guards and other infantry units for service at Tangier, which had come to this country as part of Catherine of Braganza's dowry. To this battalion the Coldstream Guards contributed two officers and 130 rank and file. Two years later the battalion returned to England, reduced by disease to barely a third of its original effective strength of 600.

When Charles II died in 1685 the new King, James II, confirmed the Foot Guards in their existing status and privileges, and they were employed in the short campaign against the Duke of Monmouth, Charles II's illegitimate son. The pikemen had now disappeared from the regiment, and bayonets were issued for the first time in 1686.

The Regiment had a conflict of loyalties in 1688 when William of Orange landed, and King James fled to the Continent. The Colonel, the aged and bellicose Earl of Craven, had to be particularly ordered by the fleeing king not to attack the Dutch troops moving to take possession of St James's and Whitehall. Indeed, James made a point of saying farewell to the officers of the Coldstream Guards at Rochester before taking ship for France.

It might have been in spite of, or because of, the regiment's obvious loyalty to the exiled King that both battalions were soon posted out of the country. In Flanders, the traditional 'cockpit of Europe', the regiment was speedily in action. In 1689 it fought against the French at Walcourt with great distinction under the command of the Earl of Marlborough, with whom the Coldstreamers were to serve on more than one later occasion. Two years of comparative inactivity followed. In 1691 King William took command of the army, and in August of the following year the regiment saw more action at the Battle of Steenkirk. In 1693, at the Battle of Landen, the Coldstreamers seem to have come under King William's personal command. They fiercely defended a position against combined French cavalry and infantry forces in a very superior strength, but the odds became too great, and the

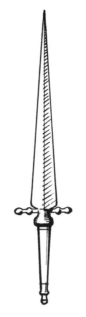

Plug-bayonet, 1680–1700
The earliest type of bayonet, adapted from the crossbow-man's knife made at Bayonne. It was fixed to the musket by insertion of the wooden grip into the muzzle. However, this proved a most unsatisfactory arrangement, for the presence of the bayonet prevented the weapon being fired; it was often difficult to unfix; and, thirdly, if it were not securely fixed, it might be dropped or left in the body of the enemy. It was in 1689 at the Battle of Killiecrankie that the plug-bayonet was largely responsible for the massacre of a British army. The bayonets had become wet and swelled in the musket barrels, with the result that not a shot could be fired against the Scots

Allies were forced to withdraw. However, a proud souvenir in the shape of a standard captured from the French Household Cavalry was carried off by the Coldstreamers.

The following year the command of the regiment was conferred on Lord Cutts, who had a tremendous reputation as a fighting soldier, and whose conduct in action had gained for him the sobriquet of 'Salamander Cutts'. He was to prove himself in command of his new regiment the following year at the siege of Namur. The Coldstream Guards, operating for the first time in a brigade of the three British Guards regiments (with the 1st Guards and the 3rd (Scots) Guards), together with a battalion of Dutch Guards, advanced into the teeth of a murderous fire from the outlying fortifications of the enemy position. Holding their fire until their musket barrels actually touched the enemy fieldworks, they delivered a devastating volley and then charged with the bayonet. They forced their way over or through the French breastworks; then, pouring over a second line of defences, they finally drove the French right up to the walls of Namur itself. This tremendous exploit was not accomplished without the heavy toll of dead and wounded this close type of fighting entailed, and the Coldstreamers suffered severely. After this action Lord Cutts was made Brigadier of the Brigade of Guards, an unprecedented honour, for no man had ever before held such an appointment.

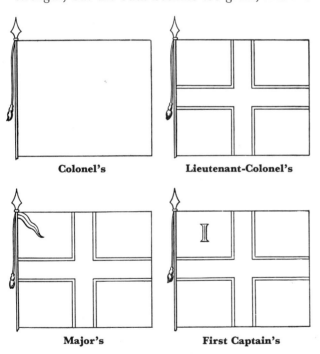

Colonel's   **Lieutenant-Colonel's**

Major's   **First Captain's**

Colours of the Coldstream Guards, 1670
In April 1669 a Wardrobe Warrant authorized the issue of twelve colours to the regiment, 'the colours of the several Captains to be distinguished by figures'. The colours were blue, plain for the Colonel's, the others bearing the red cross of St George edged in white as for the Lieutenant-Colonel. The Major had a white flame in the canton, and the Captain's colours bore the appropriate roman numerals in white. The cords and tassels were of blue, red and white silk

Ring-bayonet, 1689–1702

The first attachment allowing the musket to be fired with the bayonet in position. The loose-fitting rings had obvious disadvantages – the bayonet was more often than not shot from the musket by the force of the blast

Following this action the regiment was employed in the continuing siege. Service in the trenches alternated with guard duty on the person of the King, until the French Commander, the famous Marshal Boufflers, surrendered to the Allies.

Until the war ended with the Peace of Ryswick on 10 September 1697 the regiment was based about Ghent, whence it returned to England in November of the same year.

1702-1781

The regiment was based in England during the early years of the War of the Spanish Succession which broke out in 1702, with their headquarters at Somerset House barracks. But several contingents of Coldstreamers participated in small Continental operations, one of them in the same year the war began: six companies were included in a provisional battalion of Guards which was involved in a singularly ill-conceived and badly executed expedition to Cadiz and Vigo in Spain. This proved totally abortive, and the Coldstreamers returned to London within a few months.

In 1704 another sea-borne expedition was mounted, the initial destination being Portugal. Four hundred men of the Coldstream Guards formed part of the British force which landed at Lisbon in September, only to be re-embarked almost at once and directed towards Gibraltar. The Coldstreamers formed a combined battalion with some 200 men of the Grenadier Guards. After having been at some risk from pursuing French men-of-war, and in fact only just escaping capture, the troops landed at Gibraltar on 20 January 1705. The French and Spanish Governments had not taken kindly to the British possession of such an important strategical feature as Gibraltar Rock, and their forces were pressing its siege most vigorously. Several all-out attempts were made by the besiegers to carry the defences, but all were foiled. Nor were counter-efforts lacking in enterprise. One well-conducted sortie destroyed a considerable stretch of the siege-works. A particularly fierce enemy attack was launched on 7th February, but the Coldstreamers stood to their defences and with other units drove off the assaulting troops with volleys of musketry. The enemy's losses were so severe that they raised the siege in April and withdrew.

The Coldstreamers – still part of the Guards composite battalion – next saw service in Spain. They occupied Barcelona throughout a French siege of the city which lasted until April 1706. A month later the battalion was moved into the province of Valencia, where it took part in the ill-starred campaign of 1707, during which the Allied leaders were sadly at odds with each other and non-cooperation was the norm. This state of affairs reached a climax at the Battle of Almanza (25 April 1707) when that portion of the Allied Army which included the Guards was met by the French and Spanish Army under the Duke of Berwick and crushingly defeated. The Coldstream Guards suffered the most cruel losses which, added to the diseases the troops had experienced in Spain, more or less terminated the career of the contingent and indeed of the battalion as a fighting force. We hear no more of it.

In the same year the legendary 'Salamander' died. There seems to have been a pretty wide divergence of opinion regarding his character, but his bravery was in no way questioned. He was succeeded as Colonel of the Coldstream Guards by Gen. Charles Churchill, brother of 'Corporal John' and a very distinguished soldier in his own right. The war in the Low Countries had been in progress for some years, and the battles of Blenheim and Ramillies had already been fought, when in 1708 the regiment was in action in the third of Marlborough's great battles – Oudenarde. On this occasion the regiment was represented by six companies, brought up to battalion strength by the addition of a number of men from the Grenadier Guards. Oudenarde was an extremely hard fight, but at the culmination of some brilliant manœuvring by Marlborough, the French under Vendôme were thoroughly beaten and driven back in disorder by the Allied troops. The Coldstreamers figured prominently after a long and exhausting forced march to reach the battlefield.

The following year reinforcements were sent out

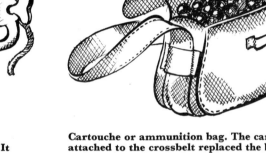

Matchlock. The operational mechanism of the musket in use during the seventeenth century. It was subject to serious drawbacks, the main faults being that it took far too long to load; the lighted slow match proclaimed to the enemy the presence of the musketeers; there was always considerable danger of ammunition being exploded accidentally by these lighted matches, while wet weather might put the whole army out of action

Cartouche or ammunition bag. The cartouche attached to the crossbelt replaced the bandoleer, and was introduced when it became clear that it was much more convenient to carry the charges readily assembled in a cartridge paper than loose on the bandoleer. Each charge consisted of the correct amount of gunpowder, and a musket ball, wrapped together in greased paper. This was rammed into the barrel in one action

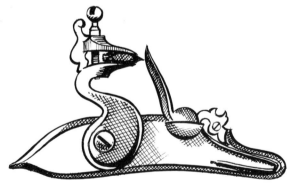

Flintlock. This firing mechanism was in use in the eighteenth century and almost up to the middle of the nineteenth. The flintlock musket was rather more safe to fire, the use of the match having been dispensed with. During the latter part of Queen Anne's reign, the word 'Tower' first appeared on locks. This indicated that the mechanism had been inspected and approved by Government officials at the Tower of London. The most popular flintlock musket was the 'Brown Bess' (below) of which varieties were in use from 1750 to 1840

to the regiment. This brought the six companies up to such strength that the composite battalion was no longer required, and in 1708 the Coldstreamers fought at Malplaquet as a separate unit.

This was by far the most bitterly fought and bloodiest of any of Marlborough's battles. Commanding the enemy was Marshal Villars, whose immense popularity with his men contributed much to the sustained defence carried on by the French. The Coldstream Guards were in the very forefront – the right centre of the front line. The French had erected field fortifications between two woods, which provided protection for their right and left flanks, and these were the scenes of the most violent fighting. A tremendous cavalry combat in the centre of the battlefield resulted in Malplaquet being another victory for Marlborough, although his army had suffered far heavier losses than had the French. The regiment was in the heat of the fighting, exchanging the point-blank musketry which the tactics and weapons of the time demanded. At the end of the long day it was recorded that, of the twenty British battalions taking part, the Coldstream Guards had sustained the heaviest losses.

Campaigning continued until the Peace of Utrecht in 1713, when once again the regiment found itself in London. The regimental strength at this time was fixed for both battalions at eighteen companies, which remained the formal establishment for some eighty years.

After the War of the Spanish Succession the regiment enjoyed a prolonged period of peacetime duties which lasted for almost thirty years. The only undertaking during this time was the employment of some companies in another amphibious operation (to Vigo) of no great moment.

On the commencement of the War of the Austrian Succession in 1742, the 1st Battalion of

George II at Dettingen, 1743, from an oil painting by John Wooten. This was the last occasion when a British monarch personally commanded an army in the field (National Army Museum)

the Coldstream Guards was sent to Flanders to join the Allied Army fighting for the cause of Maria Theresa of Austria. In the following year King George II took command in person, the last occasion when a British monarch commanded troops in the field. Led by the King, the Allied Army was retiring along the northern side of the River Main when they found their progress barred by a French force at Dettingen (27 June 1743). At the same time another French army was coming up fast in the rear, and to add to the Allied predicament they were under fire from French artillery on the other side of the river. The position was not an enviable one and the resulting battle was an untidy, scrambling sort of affair with the honours going mainly to the British cavalry. The French were driven off, but the Coldstream Guards forming part of the rearguard were little more than spectators, although keeping the French at a respectful distance.

For some two years the Coldstreamers lived through the uneventful round of camp and garrison duties at Brussels and Ghent. Then early in 1745 the Duke of Cumberland was appointed to command the Allied Army and at once prepared to take the field against the French, now under Marshal Saxe. In April the campaign opened with Saxe's laying siege to the important fortress of Tournai, whereupon Cumberland and his associated generals determined to march to its relief. On 11th May Saxe and Cumberland faced each other at Fontenoy, where the French had taken up a very strong position. Saxe had increased its natural defence potential by throwing up redoubts at various positions along the line and filling them with men and guns. With the armies in position, the British portion of Cumberland's army faced that section of an 'L'-shaped French line which lay between Fontenoy itself and the Wood of Barri nearby, both occupied by the enemy. After attacks on both extremities of this line failed it was decided to launch an infantry attack, although it must have been obvious that, with Fontenoy and the wood on the flanks held in strength by the enemy, this would be a very dangerous undertaking. In two long lines the mass of scarlet-clad infantry moved off up the slight slope towards the French, the Coldstream Guards in the right centre of the front line, flanked by

Officer's spontoon, 1700–92

The spontoon, or half-pike, was the weapon of all company officers except those of light companies. Officers also carried a sword, but ceased to carry the spontoon in 1792 when it was issued to sergeants to replace the halberd

their comrades of the 1st Guards and the Scots Guards. The two lines advanced steadily for over half a mile, coming under increasingly heavy cannon fire and musketry. Men began to fall everywhere, but the regiments maintained their forward progress, each unit meticulously keeping its dressing and filling up the gaps in the ranks as they appeared. On they went, scourged by the flanking fire from Fontenoy and the Wood of Barri, until they were only thirty yards from the long lines of French infantry. These lines included some of the most renowned French units – the Gardes Françaises, the Gardes Suisses, and infantry regiments such as Courten and Aubeterre. A hasty volley swept the British but it must have been discharged by nervous and apprehensive men, taken aback at the sight of the grimly silent line of red-clad soldiery facing them but a short distance away, and it did less damage than might have been expected. The next second a perfect hurricane of fire struck the French as the British volleys thundered and roared along the line.

In that moment the entire French front line was swept away. Whole regiments were destroyed by what must surely have been the most destructive volley in the whole course of eighteenth-century warfare. Nearly 700 men of the Gardes Françaises fell. Forward pressed the British infantry, a further 300 yards into the heart of the

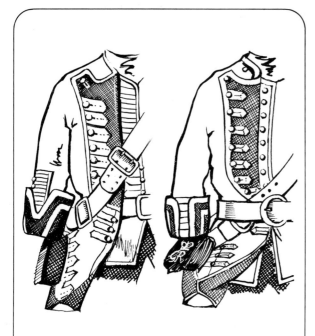

Typical infantry soldiers' coats of the middle eighteenth century. In the 1742 pattern the waist-belt is worn over the coat, while under it in that of 1750. Cuffs are very full and the buff belts broad and heavy

1st Battalion was engaged in a landing on the French coast. In July 1760 the 2nd Battalion, brigaded with two other Guards battalions under Maj.-Gen. Julius Caesar, left for Germany to serve in the Allied Army under Prince Ferdinand of Brunswick.

At the Battle of Wilhelmsthal in June 1762, when forming part of a column under the Marquis of Granby, the Coldstream Guards were involved in most bitter fighting with some crack French Grenadiers, causing many of the latter to lay down their arms. On 21st September in the same year at the action of the Brücke Mühle, the French fought with special gallantry to capture an important hill named the Amoneberg, after Prince Ferdinand's failure to provide adequate support for the troops holding it. This was the last engagement of the Coldstreamers in the Seven Years War, which ended soon after; and in the following year the Coldstream Guards returned to England.

In the next decade the Coldstreamers again

French position, but now they found themselves isolated. With neither flank nor rear support the situation changed radically; and what had seemed imminent victory now became probable defeat as Marshal Saxe flung counter-attack after counter-attack at the diminishing British regiments. Steadily and without panic, the infantry began to fall back, maintaining perfect order and discipline but leaving the Fontenoy slope strewn thickly with red-coated dead and wounded – 250 from the Coldstream Guards alone. It was the first of a series of defeats that the Allies were to suffer at the hands of the brilliant Saxe.

Shortly after Fontenoy the great bulk of the army made a hasty return to England to deal with the Jacobite invasion of the Young Pretender, Prince Charles Edward Stuart. The '45 Rebellion was put down in the following year, and in 1747 the 2nd Battalion of the Coldstream Guards was sent back to the Low Countries where it remained until the Peace of Aix-la-Chapelle in 1749. Nine years of home service followed, until the war with France was renewed in 1758, and in that year the

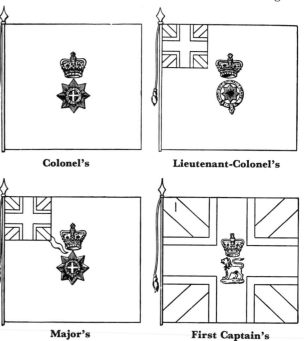

Colonel's   **Lieutenant-Colonel's**

Major's   **First Captain's**

Colours of the Coldstream Guards, 1750

The 1746 Colour Book shows the crimson Colonel's colour displaying the Garter Star and crown, the Lieutenant-Colonel's an eight-pointed star within the Garter, ensigned with the crown and bearing a small Union in the upper corner, and the Major's colour the same as for the Colonel but with the small Union having a gold flame springing from the corner. The Captains' Union colours – the cross of St George and white cross of St Andrew – displayed each a company badge with the crown in the centre, and a company numeral in gold roman figures in the canton

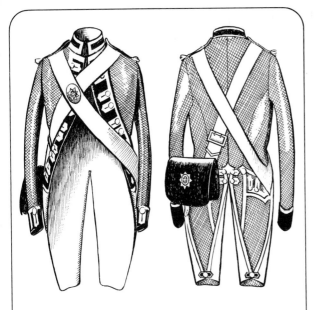

Battalion corporal's coat (front and rear), 1788

The coat of a corporal in the Coldstreamers at the end of the eighteenth century was made of red cloth, with dark blue facings, white lace and a stand-up collar. The buttons are pewter and the junction of the skirts blue, with white lace. As a corporal only one fringed epaulette is worn on the right shoulder. A private's coat would be identical, but without fringe on either epaulette

was the same procedure: the Coldstreamers held their fire in the classic British manner until close to the enemy so that the first volley could do the maximum damage, and then completed the operation by charging home with the bayonet. Lord Cornwallis, the Commander-in-Chief, conveyed to the regiment his appreciation of its behaviour.

But the surrender of Lord Cornwallis at Yorktown marked the end of hostilities, and the establishment of the new American republic. It had not been a war which allowed the British soldier to show himself to his best advantage, and it must have been a relief to board the transports back to England.

prepared for war, this time in America, where the colonists had decided to opt for independence. As on previous occasions, a composite battalion was formed from the three regiments of Foot Guards, with the Coldstream Regiment contributing nine officers and nearly 300 men as well as the commanding officer, Colonel Edward Mathew. On arrival in America the contingent was divided into two battalions with Mathew as Brigadier. During the next few years the battalions saw a great deal of arduous and exhausting service, as well as much hard fighting. In June 1778 at Freehold the Coldstreamers, under Sir Henry Clinton, won great praise for carrying out a successful attack on a most stubbornly defended enemy line, in such heat that men dropped in their tracks from exhaustion. The regiment was also represented at the White Plains fighting, and distinguished itself at the fording of the Catawba. The men waded through the swiftly flowing river, holding their fire under a hail of musket balls until they reached the further bank; then they drove off the enemy with a rapid succession of well-aimed volleys. At Guildford it

Private (light company), 1792, from a painting by E. Dayes

The light company was one of the two flank companies of the regiment, the other being the grenadier company. Both flank companies were distinguished by the large, winged epaulettes, and light company troops wore breeches of buckskin, strapped beneath their boots and buttoned up each side to just below the knee. No gaiters were worn. The light troops acted as skirmishers and were presumed more nimble than their fellows (National Army Museum)

The Napoleonic Wars

The French Revolution, breaking into its full fury with the execution of Louis XVI in 1793, marked the beginning of nearly a quarter of a century of almost continuous fighting against the armies of Revolutionary and Napoleonic France. With Britain firmly committed to the anti-French alliance, the Guards regiments were put on a war footing and the first battalions of all three regiments mobilized. At the same time their grenadier companies were united into a single grenadier battalion to form a species of *élite* body of shock troops (a common arrangement throughout the eighteenth century). Later a fourth company consisting of the light troops of all three second battalions was added to the grenadiers, the whole forming a complete battalion.

The Guards Brigade was quickly moved to the Continent, and was posted to face the northern frontier of France where, on 8th May, the Coldstreamers went into action. Flung into the attack against well-defended French entrenchments – which had already repulsed three assaults by other Allied troops – the 600 Coldstreamers went in with gusto. At first they drove the enemy back, but combined musketry and cannon fire from a cleverly concealed flanking battery caused heavy losses and forced them to retire with 70 casualties.

Sergeant (centre company), 1792, from a painting by E. Dayes

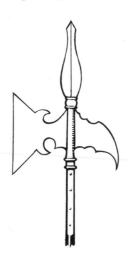

This, and other paintings by Dayes, show the orders of dress for the Coldstream Guards and provide one of the best sources of material for the period. The long halberd (left) of the 1700–92 pattern is carried, and it was with this weapon that sergeants would form up around the colours to ward off a cavalry attack. Out of action, its uses were primarily for dressing the troops and marking when on parade. In 1792 sergeants ceased to carry the halberd, and it was replaced by a half-pike or spontoon, carried by N.C.O.s of grenadier and centre companies only. Light company N.C.O.s carried rifled muskets. The half-pike was not used after 1830 (National Army Museum)

The Coldstreamers were next employed at the siege of Valenciennes but were soon detached to join the force detailed to besiege Dunkirk. This part of the campaign was grossly mismanaged and uncoordinated, with plans being made only to be abandoned. On 18th August the Guards had to go to the assistance of some Dutch troops under severe enemy pressure at Lincelles. The Dutch made something of a precipitate retreat, leaving the British to face the music; but, advancing with levelled bayonets, the Coldstreamers and the rest of the brigade dashed at the French and sent them off in great confusion.

The two years which followed were miserable ones for the British Army in the Low Countries, with lack of provisions, poor clothing and frequent bad weather. Diseases reached epidemic proportions and men died in hundreds from illness and exposure. Medical supplies and facilities were more or less non-existent, and men being conveyed in wagons to rudimentary hospitals sometimes froze to death before they arrived. Finally there was no option but to abandon operations and a painful retreat was made to the port of Bremen. There the Coldstream Guards embarked, and reached England in May 1795.

The Coldstreamers returned to Holland in 1799, forming part of two Guards brigades which fought with distinction at the Helder, Bergen and Alkmaar, before being recalled to England.

Calls upon the regiment for active service followed each other rapidly and in 1800 the 1st

Left: Sergeant (grenadier company), 1790
Right: Private (grenadier company), 1790

Although a flintlock musket was carried at this period, the match case was still worn on the crossbelt purely as an ornament (National Army Museum)

Battalion sailed with the expedition to be made against Vigo. When this proved impracticable the fleet continued on into the Mediterranean, bound for Egypt, for the troops to form part of Sir Ralph Abercromby's army. There followed tedious months at sea until a landing was made at Aboukir Bay on 8 March 1801. The disembarkation was hotly disputed by the French occupation forces, and the Coldstreamers in their landing barges came under intense fire from all arms as they approached the beaches. The operation, begun during the hours of darkness, was carried out with the greatest discipline, the men sitting courageously in their frail craft as the water around erupted with shot and shell. Once on the beaches the Coldstreamers shouldered muskets and advanced resolutely up the sandhills, whose summits were crowned by strong enemy forces. The fighting was severe, but ultimately the British bayonets carried the day, the French were driven off and

the beachhead firmly established. During the next few days the army moved forward and, on meeting the French drawn up before Alexandria, set to work to fortify a position facing them. The expected attack came on 21st March, in the early hours. The Coldstreamers were on the extreme left of the British line and it was on this flank that fighting began, but almost at once the whole line was under strong and sustained attack. The Coldstreamers came under heavy canister fire which caused many casualties. Following this came an infantry assault which they drove back with heavy losses to the enemy, and at length the French broke off the fighting and withdrew in good order. The battle cost the life of Abercromby, who died of wounds on 28th March.

Alexandria surrendered on 1st September, and at the conclusion of the campaign the Coldstream Guards returned to England, with a short stay at Malta *en route*.

Left: Drummer (centre company), 1792; right: Private (centre company), 1792 (National Army Museum)

Two expeditions were made by the 1st Battalion during 1805 and 1807, the first to Bremen and the second to Denmark; but on both occasions they returned to England without having been actively engaged. In January 1809, however, the battalion – numbering some 1,100 officers and men – brigaded with the 1st Battalion Scots Guards, sailed for the Spanish peninsula, for the long series of operations which were to culminate four years later with Wellington's drive across the Pyrenees into France. In May the brigade was at Coimbra in Portugal, the starting-point for the British advance to Oporto. In the following action the light company of the Coldstream Guards was first across the River Douro, before the whole regiment united to chase the French through the streets and into the open country beyond. The enemy made good their retreat by burning their baggage and escaping on goat tracks through the frontier mountains.

On 27th and 28th July the regiment formed part of the centre of the British Army facing a powerful French force at Talavera. During the two days of the battle, three concentrated attacks were made on the British line by almost the entire French infantry. At one point only Wellington's quick action in moving his small reserve prevented the complete dislocation of his line. Another time the Coldstreamers, having halted an enemy thrust, rushed forward with the bayonet into range of enemy cannon fire, and counter-attack by foot and horse. Despite heavy losses they restored the situation, and after regrouping they returned to the offensive with a rush, driving the enemy before them. The regiment's casualties were very high, however, with 36 officers and men killed, and 263 wounded. Wellington, never lavish with his praise, included in his General Order on the battle a description of the charge as 'a most gallant one'.

Two further companies of the Coldstream Guards, this time from the 2nd Battalion, came out to Spain in March 1810 and were sent to reinforce the British garrison at Cadiz.

With Marshal Masséna, one of Napoleon's ablest paladins, in command, the remorseless tide of the French Army now rolled across Spain until, on 26th September, it was halted by Wellington on the rocky slopes of Busaco. For two days the British held off the French attacks, with the Cold-

streamers active on their stretch of front, until their position was outflanked and they drew back to the fortified lines of Torres Vedras in Portugal. Over the next few months frequent sorties were made to keep the French on the alert, and in November 1810 the Coldstreamers participated in a very successful harrying attack. At last, with all provisions exhausted and his army reduced to desperate straits, Masséna began to retreat on 5 March 1811. Efforts were made to convert his withdrawal into a rout. The Coldstream Guards took a prominent part in the pursuit, which was so close and sustained that the French had to destroy all their baggage and much ammunition when making good their crossing of the River Coa.

Meantime, on 4 March 1811, the two companies of the 2nd Battalion from Cadiz had had a splendid fight at the Battle of Barrosa, taking part in a dashing charge which overwhelmed a strong force of French and drove them from the field.

On 3rd May Masséna turned at bay and delivered a series of tremendous attacks on Wellington, whose army was about the village of Fuentes d'Onoro. Assault after assault broke upon the British, but all were beaten off. After a day's respite the battle was renewed on the 5th. The Coldstreamers were posted at some distance from the main scene of action and consequently suffered only slightly, although at one stage having to drive off with musketry a French cavalry charge. At length Masséna, not daring to maintain the struggle and running short of ammunition, withdrew on 8th May with far heavier losses than Wellington.

Coming out of winter quarters for the 1812 campaign, the regiment was employed in siege operations – first at Cuidad Rodrigo during January, then for the murderous business of the siege of Badajos, which fell on 6th April.

The summer was occupied with the operations against Marshal Marmont, a clever and accomplished soldier now in command of the French Army. The opposing armies, after some preliminary marching and manoeuvring, came to grips at Salamanca on 22nd July. For once Wellington abandoned his traditional defensive role, and at precisely the correct moment sent his army like a thunderbolt into the French as they were engaged in a dangerous flank march across the British front. Much of the heaviest fighting took place about the village of Arapiles where the light company of the Coldstream Guards was subjected to repeated attacks. They held out stoutly, and the regiment was the subject of a highly laudatory reference by Wellington in his report on the battle. Altogether it was a tremendous defeat for the French who lost 12,000 men in killed, wounded and prisoners, as well as many guns and two of the cherished regimental 'eagles'.

The year's campaigning ended with the unsuccessful siege of Burgos, after which the army returned to winter quarters.

In the spring of 1813 the British were quickly on the move again, and on 21st June the victory of Vittoria was the immediate preliminary to a crossing of the Pyrenees. To secure his rear, Wellington laid siege in August to the great fortress of San Sebastian, a castle surrounded by the town of San Sebastian which itself was protected by stout walls. As soon as a breach had been opened in the town walls by artillery bombardment a detachment of two officers, two sergeants, a drummer and fifty men of the Coldstream Guards volunteered to take part in storming it. The 'forlorn hope', as it was appropriately named, was the first unit into the maelstrom of fire blasting through the narrow confines of the breach. Time after time the men forced their way over the heaps of rubble and ruined walls to mount the defences, but time after time they had to give way as their ranks were swept by musket fire. Finally on 31st August the defence cracked, the British poured in, and the town was taken. The castle surrendered some days later, but more than half the Coldstreamer detachment had fallen dead or wounded.

The battalion rejoined the field army now pressing forward through the mountain barrier, and before long France lay before the invading army. First came the crossing of the Nive, then the Nivelle, and the British columns were marching hard for Bayonne. By 23rd March the troops were approaching the city, but first the River Adour had to be crossed on pontoons. Among the leading troops to cross, the light company of the Coldstreamers, together with men of the Scots Guards, were attacked by French infantry, who after a volley came rushing in with fixed bayonets. After a hard fight the French retreated, leaving the

British to consolidate the crossing during that night and the following day. By 27th March the blockade of Bayonne was complete. This was the Coldstream Guards' last action of the war. The Battle of Orthez on 27th February had already been won by Wellington, and on 10th April he attacked the French at Toulouse. It was a costly encounter, more so to the British than to the French, but it was nevertheless a victory – the last of the Peninsular War. In July 1814 the Coldstream Guards returned to England after nearly six years of the hardest campaigning the regiment had ever experienced.

Meanwhile, on 13 December 1813, six companies of the 2nd Battalion had been sent to Holland. On 8 and 9 March 1814 they were in action against the strong fortress of Bergen-op-Zoom, an ill-judged venture; the British forces suffered extremely heavy losses, and the attempt was a failure. On 4th August, however, the six companies were moved to Brussels and shortly afterwards the battalion was completed by the arrival of the headquarters component and the

First State Colour of the Coldstream Guards

In addition to the ordinary colours, the Coldstream Guards have two much larger colours – the First State Colour and the Second State Colour. The First was presented to the regiment by Queen Charlotte (Consort of George III), and consists of two sheets of crimson taffeta, embroidered in gold with the exception of the sphinxes, which are silver. The crown and Garter Star are in full colour, and the blue scroll below the central device bears the word 'Egypt' worked in purl and spangle. Both the First and Second State Colours were carried on pikes

four other companies from England. It was thus happily at full strength when the news sped across Europe that Napoleon had escaped from banishment on the island of Elba and had arrived in Paris. Again battle had to be joined and at once the battalion was moved to a more advanced position at Enghien. There it remained until 16 June 1815 when the fury of Napoleon's onslaught fell upon the scattered British and Prussian Armies.

Everywhere the roads of Belgium resounded with the thud of boots and horses' hooves, and the iron rumble of guns as the troops poured along the dusty highways to their concentration positions. At Quatre Bras Wellington grimly held off a furious attack by Marshal Ney while his supporting brigades and divisions made forced marches to join him. Roused before daybreak, the Coldstream Guards – forming the 2nd Guards Brigade with the Scots Guards – pushed tirelessly along through the dawn mist at a great pace. They marched twenty-five miles through the heat in full marching order to arrive at Quatre Bras at 4.00 p.m. For hours the men with Wellington had held on under continual attack from cavalry and infantry, and the issue was in the balance. But when the Guards arrived the scene changed, defence became offence, and in support of the 1st Guards Brigade the Coldstreamers surged forward. It was the turning-point of the battle, and everywhere the battered enemy fought to the point of exhaustion.

But the success at Quatre Bras was counterbalanced by Napoleon defeating the Prussians at Ligny on the same day. When news of this was brought to Wellington on the 17th, he gave orders for retreat to the Waterloo position. There, on the morning of 18th June, the British general drew up his somewhat heterogeneous army to meet the last grand attack of the Emperor of the French.

On the right front of the Allied position the farm – or chateau as it can also be called – of Hougoumont had been occupied by the light companies of the four Guards battalions, that from the Coldstream Guards being stationed in the buildings and gardens of the farm under Lieut.-Col. Macdonell. Loopholes had been made in the walls, and the gates barricaded. The remainder of the Coldstream battalion was on a

Officers, Coldstream Guards, 1821, from a painting by Dighton

These belong to a battalion company, thus wearing the shako as headgear. It was not until 1832 that the 'regiment entire' was ordered to wear the bearskin cap, formerly the prerogative of the grenadier company. Left: lieutenant in half dress, wearing undress coat and hessian boots; right: lieutenant-colonel in full dress, his rank indicated by the two gold-fringed epaulettes. All captains in the Foot Guards were automatically given the rank of lieutenant-colonel (National Army Museum)

ridge just behind Hougoumont. Shortly after 11.00 a.m. the first attack on the farm was made by troops of Napoleon's brother Jerome. It was intended by the Emperor to be a diversionary move, but was converted into an all-out effort by the young man burning to make a name for himself, and continuous assaults broke upon the farm buildings for many hours. Skirmishers crept through the undergrowth of the nearby woods to fire at short range. Some Nassau infantry taking part in the defence were driven off, but Macdonell and his Coldstreamers counter-attacked immediately. They gained at least partial relief, but soon masses of French infantry occupied all the outbuildings of the farm and actually burst open the great gate and broke into the main courtyard. Again Macdonell and his men were on the scene and managed to close the gate.

At this point reinforcements, including a company of Coldstreamers, came to the hard-pressed defenders and, together with the original garrison, they charged and drove back the French. The officer commanding the Coldstream Guards, Col. Woodford, brought four more companies of his regiment into the fight. He made a truly desperate attempt to drive the French out of the wood about the farm, but the odds were too great and the Coldstreamers had to fall back into the buildings. Hour after hour the battle continued, with volleys at close range and hand-to-hand fighting with bayonet and musket-butt. The defence hung on courageously throughout the long day, half blinded by the great clouds of billowing smoke.

Evening came at last and with it the defeat of the French Imperial Guard. The French began to fall back, slowly at first but then in complete disintegration. Hougoumont had been held but at a fearful cost – the Coldstream Guards had lost 8 officers and 300 other ranks killed or wounded.

The battle over, the regiment took part in the advance on Paris which was entered in July. It remained there until February 1816 when it was posted to Cambrai. The regiment returned to London in November 1818.

The Crimea

The period of European peace following the Battle of Waterloo lasted for nearly forty years. During this time the Coldstreamers had only one short period of operational service: the 2nd Battalion was sent to Canada in 1838 to assist in dealing with a minor rebellion which had broken out in the province of Lower Canada, inhabited almost exclusively by French settlers. Discontent had been brewing for some time, and in November 1837 this flared into open revolt under a certain Papineau; at the same time another rising occurred in Upper Canada. These events greatly disturbed the British Government, and 800 men of the Coldstream Guards, together with the 2nd Battalion Grenadier Guards, sailed from Plymouth on 17th April and arrived in Canada on 11th May.

They landed to find that there was nothing for them to do, the uprisings having already been effectively put down by the troops *in situ*; and although there was a disturbance not far from Montreal in November the Coldstreamers were not called upon. The battalion remained in Quebec until 1842 although there was little but garrison duties to occupy them. Some found life in Canada to their liking, and a number of discharges on the spot were permitted. It was made known that 'this extensive indulgence' had been assented to 'in consequence of the very exemplary manner in which the Guards have conducted themselves during the time they have performed Colonial service in North America'. Thus spake the voice of military high command in the nineteenth century.

In 1854 came the outbreak of the war with Russia – whose Czar had ten years before inspected the 2nd Battalion Coldstream Guards and spoken of them in glowing terms. Britain, France and Turkey (unusual allies) decided upon an invasion of the Crimea with a view to seizing the great naval base at Sebastopol. In February a Guards brigade which included the 1st Battalion of the Coldstreamers was put on a war footing, and 900 of the battalion sailed on the 22nd of the month for Malta. There the brigade was concentrated under Maj.-Gen. Bentinck of the Coldstream Guards, forming with Sir Colin Campbell's Highland Brigade the 1st Division under the Duke of Cambridge. From Malta the next stop was Scutari; after six weeks there – during which time the more knowing marked the significant lack of transport and the inadequacy of medical supplies – a landing was made at Varna in Bulgaria, where the business of concentrating and organizing the entire Allied Army was undertaken.

Coldstream Guards Band, *c.* 1830

The negro musician carrying the 'Jingling Johnnie', or set of Turkish bells, was characteristic of all guards bands at the time. The Coldstream Guards had three negro musicians as far back as 1790. The last was discharged by the regiment about 1840.

Conditions were bad, and over fifty men of the battalion died from typhoid and cholera. Finally an embarkation was made for the long-awaited invasion, and after some further delay a landing was made on 14th September, some twenty-five miles from Sebastopol. The British force was on the left, the Turks on the right, while the French formed the centre. The Russians offered no resistance, only a few patrolling Cossacks watched the disembarkation. The same day the Guards Brigade marched some three miles inland and bivouacked for the night.

Within a few days, however, the main enemy became apparent – the variety of diseases which were to cause far heavier losses than the guns and muskets of the Russians – and everywhere men began to fall out with debility and recurring cholera.

On 20th September the first contact was made with the Russian forces. Some 40,000 men were stationed on the crest of a strong, hilly position in front of which ran the River Alma. The French crossed the river and scaled the steep slopes facing them with little opposition, for the Russians had presumed them impassable and had covered them with only the minimum troops. The leading regiments of the British moved up the easier slopes which were swept by concentrated enemy fire. Numerically, the Russian Army was slightly inferior to that of the Allies, but the British section

faced the greater part of it. The attack was launched by the Light Division and the 2nd Division, while the 1st Division with the Coldstream Guards waited in support with long-range roundshot leaping and bounding through their ranks. The order for them to move finally came and at once the Coldstreamers started across the Alma. Having reached the further side in some disorder they waited until, with parade-ground precision, their markers were called out to the front. The men formed up on them, dressed their ranks, and the advance then proceeded in a manner that would not bring discredit upon the Guards.

There was intense fighting going on across the crest of the hill with the Russians hanging on to their position with great tenacity. But now the Coldstreamers were sent forward up the slope with their drums rattling and the colours borne high by their ensigns, firing as they advanced until they reached the crest. Volley after volley crashed into the massed Russians, doing tremendous execution. At last the enemy wavered. At this, with a tremendous cheer, the Coldstreamers levelled their bayonets, and drove forward to send the Russians reeling from the field in disorder. The Coldstreamers suffered only a few casualties; the other regiments of the brigade had many more. The Russians retreated from the Battle of the Alma in confusion, but there was no pursuit.

Following the Alma a partial approach was made to Sebastopol, but time was wasted before the blockade got properly under way. Throughout October the Coldstream Guards were engaged in entrenchment work, supplying troops for the construction of gun batteries, working parties and guards to hold off sorties from the garrison.

Meantime Russian reinforcements continued to arrive in the Crimea and on 25th October the Battle of Balaclava was fought, with results too well known to recapitulate, the infantry engaged in the investment of Sebastopol being too far away to make any effective intervention, although the Guards did march out but were not engaged. The incidence of sickness was rapidly increasing throughout the army, not least in the Coldstream Guards, and dozens of men were admitted every week to the makeshift hospitals.

At dawn on 5th November, however, routine

was rudely disturbed when the Russians attacked, achieving almost complete surprise. Heavy snow lay everywhere and there was a thick mist when the enemy came on in dense columns. The greatest weight of the offensive fell on a thin line of British troops on Inkerman Ridge. To the rear of the ridge lay the Coldstream Guards in a support position. The storm of the attack fell first on several British line regiments; guns were lost and retaken, but in less than three-quarters of an hour the enemy had been forced back. The Coldstream Guards took advantage of a short lull to move up into the line, but simultaneously the Russians launched a second attack and gained a hold on the plateau forming the main Inkerman Ridge. So as the Guards came up they immediately counter-attacked against deadly enemy fire. With a storm of musket balls smashing into the British ranks, the men of the Guards regiments lost touch with their commanders, and without battalion or company control fought in small isolated groups under subalterns or sergeants. They were greatly outnumbered and, as one officer said later, the struggle was 'hand to hand, foot to foot, muzzle to muzzle, butt end to butt end'. Further confusion to both sides was caused by the fog, and often pursuers of broken enemy units would run into point-blank fire from reinforcements which seemed to appear from nowhere.

Further British infantry regiments came up at length to assist the hard-pressed Guards, though some of these fresh troops advanced over-boldly and had to fight their way back to the ridge after being cut off. With the arrival of British and French reserve artillery the Russian attacks came to an end, although a number of eager Coldstreamers fell in on the right of some French infantry to join with them in a counter-attack. By 1.00 p.m. the enemy was in retreat. Fatigue and heavy losses prevented any pursuit and the British position remained on the Inkerman Ridge.

The losses of the Coldstream Guards had been the severest of any regiment. Only four unwounded officers answered roll call at the end of the battle, and the battalion's total casualties were 84 killed and 123 wounded. The trials of the wounded had only just begun, for the congested and inefficient hospitals allowed many men to perish whose lives might have been saved by proper medical care.

Inkerman was the last major field engagement of the war, but throughout the appalling winter that followed the troops suffered almost as much as they had done in action. For months the Coldstream Guards were in the Sebastopol trenches before being moved out to rest and reorganize at Balaclava. The battalion returned to the trenches in June 1855, and took part in a determined assault on the fortress after a series of bombardments. But the British were unable to capture the massive defence works known as the Redan. The other key point of the defence system, the Malakoff Redoubt, was captured by the French on 8 September 1855, and the same night the fortress was evacuated by the Russians. It was in effect the end of the war, and when the Treaty of Paris was signed on 30 March 1856 the Coldstream Guards returned to England.

Coldstream Guards at the Battle of the Alma, 20 September 1854 (Mary Evans Picture Library)

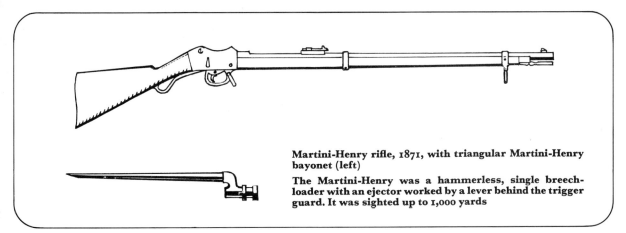

Martini-Henry rifle, 1871, with triangular Martini-Henry bayonet (left)

The Martini-Henry was a hammerless, single breech-loader with an ejector worked by a lever behind the trigger guard. It was sighted up to 1,000 yards

Of the 2,060 men who had served with the battalion in the Crimea, 699 were killed or died of wounds or disease. It was a heavy price to pay for the little that the war had accomplished.

Egypt, Sudan, and South Africa

It was not until 1882 that the regiment again saw active service. In that year, the revolt of Arabi Pasha against Turkish rule in Egypt raised a considerable threat to British interests on the Nile. After the refusal of the French to act in concert with the British, and severe rioting in Alexandria, it was determined to send an expedition to restore the situation. Gen. Sir Garnet Wolseley was appointed to the command of the British forces,

and as part of a Guards brigade the 2nd Battalion of the Coldstream Guards, some 750 strong, arrived at Alexandria on 13th August. The brigade concentrated at Ramleh. From the outset it had seemed that the enemy would make a stand at Tell el Kebîr, on the road to Cairo, and the British Army moved forward to Ismâ'ilîa.

After some sporadic fighting the entire force was concentrated at Kassassin on 12th September, ready to strike at the enemy grouped some eight miles further on at Tell el Kebîr. Before dusk the regiments began to take up their positions for the night approach, and at 1.30 a.m. the march began across the silent desert. They marched all night in total darkness, and the leading British troops rushed the Egyptian lines at first light, about 5.00 a.m. The defences were penetrated at once and the enemy quite overwhelmed. The Coldstreamers came up fast in support under a heavy if ill-directed fire. They were just in time to complete the clearing of the works, losing only a handful of men in the process. It was an unqualified victory. In less than a fortnight control had been re-established throughout Egypt, and after six weeks in Cairo the Coldstreamers returned to England in November.

Two years later the Coldstream Guards were back in Egypt, this time as a result of the religious disturbances engineered by the Mahdi, a fanatical Moslem leader. In October 1884 the first draft of Coldstreamers consisted of ninety-two officers and men who were to join a camel corps destined to assist in the relief of General Gordon, who was besieged at Khartoum in the Sudan. The relief column, including the Guards Camel Regiment, started from Korti on 30th December. There was a fierce action with dervishes at Abou Klea, when the violence of the enemy attack was quite tremendous, but the British managed to fight them off. Further attacks made to impede the progress of the force were more easily dealt with. But the effort was in vain for it was learned that Khartoum had fallen and Gordon had been killed. The relief force had been sent a month too late.

A powerful force was assembled for the following year's campaign, and early in the spring the 1st Battalion Coldstream Guards left for Egypt. The battalion arrived on 8 March 1885 at Suakin to form part of what must have been one of the earliest Commonwealth forces, for it included Indian troops and Australian infantry and artillery. Although it housed Army Headquarters, Suakin was in a constant alarm from Arab infiltrators who crept past sentries at night and murdered soldiers as they slept. About 7,000 dervishes were concentrated at Tamai, a village about sixteen miles south-west of Suakin, while another 1,000 were located at Hasnin, from whence came the night marauders. On 20th March an expedition was mounted against Hasnin with the Coldstreamers taking part. The attack was successful, the battalion had only a few casualties, and no further intruders came from this direction.

The advance was now directed against Tamai, centre of the enemy resistance, and for several days there was a great deal of confused fighting between Tamai and Suakin. The enemy were adept at concealment in the scrub and undergrowth, and more than once fell upon British troops with the advantage of surprise. The fighting centred at a place called Tofrek, and on 23rd March the Coldstreamers moved up to reinforce the British encampment there. After a lengthy fire the dervishes came in to close quarters in one of their terrifying charges. The Coldstreamers coolly held their fire until the enemy were close at hand, and then fired a deadly volley into their ranks. Only a few reached the British, to perish on their bayonets.

By now enemy activity was lessening and, after some ponies had arrived, reconnaissances made by mounted infantry detachments found only scattered parties of dervishes. Later a camel corps took over this duty, with thirty men seconded from

the Coldstream Guards. Further convoy duty was the lot of the Coldstreamers, and sporadic engagements continued until 2nd April when Tamai was occupied. The Coldstreamers then returned to Suakin and after six weeks there went on to Alexandria and Ramleh. They returned to England in September.

In 1897, during a period of peace, the regiment was augmented by the addition of a 3rd Battalion. Colours were presented to the new battalion by Queen Victoria in July 1898. The creation of a third battalion stemmed from a plan to quarter a Guards battalion at Gibraltar, and the 1st Battalion Coldstream Guards left for that fortress on 10 March 1899. But they were not allowed to remain for long at Gibraltar. During the summer

Tropical helmet, 1899–1900
The white Wolsely foreign service helmet with white puggaree was worn by officers and men alike. In 1899 when going into active service in khaki uniform, a khaki cover was worn over the helmet by rank and file. Officers, however, purchased helmets of their own made entirely from khaki. During service in Egypt a brass chain and spike of bright metal mounted on a bright dome base were worn

of 1899 relations between the British Government and the Transvaal grew increasingly strained, and as a precaution a Brigade of Guards was earmarked for foreign service. War was indeed declared on 12th October, and eight days later the 2nd Battalion embarked at Southampton for South Africa. The 1st Battalion sailed from Gibraltar for the same destination about a week later, and both arrived at Cape Town in mid-November, within a few days of each other. By 18th November they were encamped at Orange River Station, forming part of the 1st Guards Brigade in Lord Methuen's 1st Division. Their traditional scarlet coats had been left behind, and the Coldstreamers paraded in khaki, with a white helmet and puggaree substituted for the bearskin. This new headgear was ornamented with a small red plume, on which officers wore a small Coldstream star in silver. To assist in camouflage, sword and bayonet blades were painted brown.

1 Musketeer, 1678
2 Pikeman, 1668
3 Drum major, 1670

MICHAEL ROFFE

A

1 Grenadier, 1684
2 Private, 1742
3 Grenadier, 1747

B

MICHAEL ROFFE

1 **Private, grenadier company (full dress)**, 1760
2 **Sergeant (half dress)**, 1789
3 **Drummer (service dress)**, 1790

1 Officer (half dress), 1790
2 Grenadier (half dress),
1808
3 Colour sergeant,
grenadier company
(half dress), 1815

D

MICHAEL ROFFE

1 Drum major (service
dress), 1815
2 Officer, flank company
(cloaked), 1815
3 Officer, grenadier
company (half dress), 1815

1 **Colour sergeant (full dress), 1831**
2 **Private (service dress), 1831**
3 **Officer (summer dress), 1831**

F

MICHAEL ROFFE

1 Pioneer corporal
(summer dress), 1831
2 Officer (winter dress),
1840
3 Private (winter dress),
1866

1 Ensign (State dress), 1970
2 Guardsman, 1970
3 Drum major (State dress), 1970

1

2

3

H

MICHAEL ROFFE

Early on 21st November the troops marched off to the relief of the besieged town of Kimberley. On the following day they arrived at Belmont's Farm, where a substantial force of Boers with some artillery was stationed. As dawn broke the following morning the British launched an attack but were met by heavy fire from the Boer sharpshooters. Initially, the Coldstream battalions were held in reserve, but were now ordered forward against a Boer-occupied 'kopje' (low hill). After a steep climb, the Coldstreamers fixed bayonets and dashed up the last few yards to the summit. They found the position empty, for the Boers had suddenly decided not to resist the charge and galloped off on their ponies.

The Boers fell back from Belmont, failed to make a stand at Graspan, and retreated to the Modder River. There they made their last attempt to hold up the army moving to the relief of Kimberley, at the point where the Modder joins the Riet. Instead of basing their defences solely upon a line of kopjes, the Boers determined to hold the river, and lined its banks with hordes of riflemen, who were concealed by the bushes and scrub along the banks. The British general, Lord Methuen, believed that the Boers were simply carrying out delaying tactics, and were about to slip away to the north; but before he could order any move his troops came under artillery fire from across the river. At the same time they were struck by a storm of rifle-fire from the invisible enemy along the river-bank. Men of the Guards fell in dozens, for there was no natural cover of which they could make use. Crawling along the ground, the 2nd Battalion came to a stop about half a mile from the river. Their right-flanking regiments – Grenadier and Scots Guards – were also brought to a halt. No proper reconnaissance of the area seemed to have been made, and when the 1st Battalion of the regiment tried to outflank the Boers on the right, they found themselves confronted unexpectedly by the broad waters of the River Riet, flowing northwards before making a sharp westerly turn to meet the Modder. An attempt was made to cross, but the few Coldstreamers who succeeded in passing through the chest-deep river were brought back. The battalion started to 'dig in' at the point where the Riet made its westerly bend, but the shallow trenches they were able to dig afforded little protection.

As the day wore on the heat became almost unbearable, and hunger and thirst added to the men's discomfort. But there was no respite until darkness. The Boers kept the 'no-man's-land' swept with rifle-fire, sometimes slackening as if to encourage an advance, but blazing up with redoubled fury at any brave spirits who attempted it. At one point two batteries of field artillery came galloping up to give close support, their guns and gun carriages bumping over the rough ground, but their fire seemed to have little effect on the well-concealed Boer infantry. It was a bitter and fruitless day and cost heavy casualties in both Coldstream battalions, including the 2nd's Commanding Officer. During the ensuing night, however, the Boers again decided to evacuate the position, and when Methuen ordered his guns to open fire next morning, it was revealed that the enemy had (fortunately) made off during the night, leaving their virtually impregnable position undefended.

After the Modder River battle the enemy did not fall back towards Kimberley, as might have been expected, but moved eastwards. Reinforced by troops from Mafeking, they decided to make another stand on the Magersfontein Heights. There, at the end of the first week in December, they had a force of nearly 9,000 men and twelve guns under their famous leader, Cronje. Methuen carried out some intensive scouting of their position and realized that the Heights were well fortified, but failed to discover a well-concealed system of trenches some 150 yards in front of the Heights. In spite of the lesson he should have learned at the Modder River, Methuen decided to make a frontal attack on Magersfontein Hill itself, the key to the Boer position. On 10th December he made a demonstration towards the southern end of the hill and, during the afternoon, an artillery bombardment of the Heights. This caused no greater inconvenience to the Boers than the wounding of three riflemen, but it gave ample notification of an imminent attack. During the night, when the troops were on their way to their start line, a tremendous thunderstorm broke upon the armies. The British advanced almost blindly in drenching rain, the only illumination coming from the sheets of lightning, and occasionally from the distant Kimberley searchlights probing the sky with their signals. By first light on the 11th the storm had passed, but the ground was very muddy when the Highland Brigade put in the first attack. Their regiments rushed bravely forward into a heavy fire from the hidden trenches in front of the Heights, but it was an unmitigated disaster. The Highlanders were stopped in their tracks. Advancing with all speed to their support, the Coldstream battalions also came quickly under rifle-fire, which mounted in intensity through the morning. The Boer snipers were particularly deadly, picking off any officer who made the slightest move. By 2.00 a.m. it was evident that no further advance could be made.

The Coldstreamers lay in what rudimentary defences they could construct, scorched and thirsty. During the night they drew back from the Heights, and next morning the Boers were still securely ensconced. The army reluctantly withdrew further to the Modder River to regroup. The Coldstream Guards indeed stayed there until 18 February 1900, by which time the Guards Brigade had been transferred to the main army of Lord Roberts. And it was in this army that they made, during the spring, the historic advance by way of Poplar Grove and Driefontein to Bloemfontein, which was entered on 13th March. The 2nd Battalion covered forty-three miles in under twenty-eight hours during the final approach, and this on half rations.

The Coldstream Guards remained in Bloemfontein until 1st May. Then, as part of the 11th Division, they left with Lord Roberts on the first stages of the march on Pretoria. There were many skirmishes with parties of Boers, especially on the Vet and Zand rivers, but losses were relatively light. Kroonstad was entered on 12th May, Johannesburg on the 31st. After a short rest the army started off for the Boer capital where, on 4th June, both battalions were engaged in the sharp fighting which was the prelude to the enemy's evacuating the city. On the following day the 2nd Battalion led the advance into Pretoria.

Although the war was to last for a long time yet, there were no further major battles for the Coldstreams. On 12th June both battalions were in the Diamond Hill action, and on 26th August they were engaged at a place called Belfast; losses were

Drum major and drummers, Coldstream Guards, c. 1900. From an original photograph (Radio Times Hulton Picture Library)

small at both places. On 27th September the battalions returned to Pretoria by rail. There the Guards Brigade split up, and both 1st and 2nd Battalions operated on anti-commando duties in Cape Colony until the end of hostilities on 31 May 1902. No major action occurred throughout this long period, but it was an exhausting duty to counter the constant raids of the elusive commandos.

The battalions arrived back at Aldershot within a few days of each other in October 1902. It would be twelve years before they again would march to battle.

World War I

On 4 August 1914 Great Britain went to war with Germany. In the scale of its operations and the number of dead and wounded, this war surpassed any previous conflict, and for the first time in British history the Government had to resort to conscription. It was a war in which traditional manœuvring – on the Western Front at least – was impossible, for from Switzerland to the Channel the fighting was confined to a mass of complex and generally almost impregnable trench systems.

Within a fortnight of the declaration of war, the three Coldstream Guards battalions were mobilized at Le Cateau in France. Like many other units, their first action was at Mons when the tremendous German offensive was rolling forward, and soon the Coldstreamers were caught up in the retreat. The first battalion to be engaged was the 3rd, their first taste of battle; they were attacked by German cavalry and infantry at Landrecies on 25th/26th August. The action took place at night and bitter hand-to-hand fighting went on for several hours before the enemy was repulsed. They were again in action at Villers-Cotterets, with the 2nd Battalion in support. The battle took place in thickly wooded country where isolated parties of Coldstreamers, on occasion cut off from the main body, forced their way through the encircling Germans under subaltern or N.C.O. command. Fighting lasted until the late afternoon, when the enemy was driven back and the British retreat continued.

The three battalions were south of the Marne when the long retreat ended and the Allied counter-attack was put in motion, with the Germans falling back all along the line. At the crossing of the Petit Morin on 8th September it was the turn of the 2nd Battalion; they made a brisk attack, capturing many prisoners and a number of machine-guns. The battalion crossed the River Aisne on 13th September, but was withdrawn to the south bank, leaving only a small bridgehead on the further side.

On 14th September the 1st Battalion was in action on the Chemin des Dames, with an attack on an enemy-held village and factory. Part of the battalion was surrounded in thick fog by strong enemy formations, but was able to cut its way out during darkness and rejoin the battalion. But it was a day of heavy loss, 11 officers and 360 other ranks killed or wounded. Thrusting forward from the Aisne, both 2nd and 3rd Battalions were heavily engaged and lost severely. By this time autumn rains were beginning to convert the area into a morass and movement was becoming next to impossible. It was stalemate for the time, and trench-digging began at once. These trenches were often turned into veritable rivers by the rain, and although no major battle occurred there was little relief from the continual raids, counter-raids, and bombing expeditions.

A few weeks after the Battle of the Aisne the Coldstream Guards were moved to Flanders, and almost at once were engaged in the 1st Battle of Ypres. On 29th October the 1st Battalion was in the line when its right-flanking neighbour regiment broke and the Germans poured through the resulting gap. Attacking the battalion from all sides, they practically destroyed it. Only a lieutenant and eighty men were able to extricate themselves. Even so, with replacements of but 100 men, the battalion returned to the line almost immediately, but again suffered badly and had to be withdrawn for reorganization. The 2nd and 3rd Battalions continued in action at the famous Polygon Wood, and the 2nd was able to withstand repeated enemy assaults in drenching rain and thick undergrowth. No further advance was possible and again the men had to entrench. On 17th November the Coldstreamers were relieved.

The winter of 1914–15 was a hideous experience.

In a wilderness of mud and water-filled shell-holes the fighting went on every day. In late December the 1st Battalion suffered casualties of almost 50 per cent at Givenchy, and in January 1915 they held off fierce German local attacks at Cuinchy. For the remainder of the winter the story was one of daily small actions against the enemy trenches, with casualties mounting steeply. In one month, without having been engaged in any major battle, the three battalions lost 20 officers and 600 other ranks.

During the summer of 1915 all the Coldstream battalions, together with the recently formed 4th (Pioneer) Battalion of the Coldstream Guards, were incorporated into the Guards Division. This was the first occasion when the regiment had mustered four battalions for active service. During the Allied offensive in September at Loos, the 1st Battalion was in the fighting about the notorious Hill 70. Advancing across open country swept by machine-gun and rifle-fire, it assaulted a heavily defended wood and drove out the German occupants. Although suffering substantial losses, the battalion held on to the position it had won. The 4th (Pioneer) Battalion was also concerned in the battle, working on the lines and constructing communication trenches. On 8th October the 3rd Battalion was in the fighting north of Loos when an N.C.O., L/Sgt. Brooks, won the Victoria Cross for clearing a party of Germans from a section of trench.

1916 was the year of the Somme. The winter had been spent in the Laventie area, with alternating spells of trench service and rest, but all the Coldstream battalions were brought south to share in the Somme offensive which opened on 1st July. Despite the preparations and the strength of the attackers, it was the most appalling waste of life. Without achieving a breakthrough the cost in casualties was measured by thousands daily. The Guards Division went into action on 15th September at Ginchy, supported by tanks, but these broke down or stuck in the thick mud. None of the enemy strongpoints had been silenced when, for the first and indeed the only time in the regiment's history, three Coldstream Guards battalions – 1st, 2nd and 3rd – advanced together in line. Very heavy losses were sustained in their advance against heavy hand-fire and artillery, and the dead and wounded, as they fell, frequently disappeared into the engulfing mud.

The first objectives were seized, but there was a serious holdup on the right flank, and the advance ground to a halt. The main resistance came from a complicated and extensive trench system called the Quadrilateral, from which a withering fire poured forth at the Coldstreamers. However, later in the day, it was penetrated and neutralized by other Guards units, and the Coldstream battalions were able to resume their forward movement. Within an hour the secondary objectives were taken and held, in spite of the most furious resistance. The three Coldstream battalions suffered crippling losses, no less than 40 officers and 1,326 rank and file killed or wounded. The Commanding Officer of the 3rd Battalion, Lieut.-Col. John Campbell, was awarded the Victoria Cross for his gallantry, rallying and encouraging his men with blasts from a hunting horn.

Despite their shattered condition the Coldstreamers were back in the line within a few days, but were relieved on 27th September when the division was withdrawn for a spell in general reserve.

The winter of 1916–17, again a hard one, was spent in the normal routine of the trenches, if normal can be considered an appropriate word. On the Somme sector weather was very bad, and the entire area had been transformed into a sea of mud where movement was impossible. In March 1917 the Germans withdrew to their system of defences named the Hindenburg Line, and in May the Guards Division moved to Flanders for the summer offensive. On 27th July the 3rd Battalion and the 4th (Pioneer) Battalion forced a crossing of the Yser Canal and established a bridgehead, which was shelled heavily by the Germans until the 31st when the main British attack was launched. The 1st Battalion was in the thick of the resultant fighting, pressing on through the stiffest opposition, in which Private Whitham (the rank of Guardsman was not instituted until 1918) gained the Victoria Cross for capturing a German machine-gun and crew single-handed. Taking over from the 1st Battalion, the 2nd pushed on for more than two miles beyond the Canal, and held the line until relieved a few days later.

After two months of rest and training, the Cold-

The Band of the Coldstream Guards changing the Guard at Buckingham Palace (Crown copyright)

streamers were back in the line at Poelcapelle. On 9th October, in spite of more torrential rain, the 2nd Battalion moved off to the attack, sometimes wading through waist-deep water in the craters. The 1st and 3rd Battalions 'leap-frogged' through their comrades to carry on a successful operation.

In November the Guards Division moved south from Flanders for the next Allied offensive, which was to be the last battle of the year – Cambrai. When a powerful German counter-attack broke through the lines and settled in the houses of Gouzeaucourt, the 2nd and 3rd Battalions advanced against this village. Without artillery support but under heavy shellfire, they dashed through the streets and cleared the Germans from the strongpoints they had made of the houses. All this day and the next the enemy made frantic efforts to retake the village but were utterly unsuccessful. On 6th December relieving troops took over. The three battalions had lost nearly 30 officers and almost 1,000 men in the fighting.

For the Coldstream Guards 1918 was marked by the great German spring offensive which came near to achieving a complete breakthrough, and the last week in March and the first in April was a period of immense peril. For ten days the three Coldstream battalions fought, dug in, marched and fought again, all in conditions of the greatest confusion, the 'fog of war' being everywhere. Then the German attack seemed to lose its impetus to some extent, but on 11th April the Guards were moved to Hazebrouck to counter yet another

thrust. Here the 3rd Battalion fought for three days against terrific odds, parties of men being cut off and attacked from all sides. Finally reinforcements arrived and what was left of the Guards 4th Brigade was united into a single provisional battalion. The 3rd Battalion had lost 12 officers and 471 other ranks in three days of fighting, and well deserved the Commander-in-Chief's commendation: 'No more brilliant exploit has taken place since the opening of the enemy's offensive....' For the culminating Allied offensive, the Guards Division on 21st August found itself on familiar ground, between Arras and Bapaume. During the first few days of the attack the 1st and 2nd Battalions had to fight hard, but the tempo of the advance was mounting and prisoners were being taken in increasing numbers. By early September the Allied guns were thundering against the Hindenburg Line, and two weeks were occupied in preparing for a break-through assault. On the crossing of the waterless Canal du Nord by the 1st Battalion against determined opposition, Victoria Crosses were won by Capt. Frisby and L/Cpl. Jackson for destroying enemy machine-gun posts. It took the whole day for the crossing to be made good, but many prisoners and much equipment was taken, although the battalion lost 150 casualties.

Between 9th October and 11th November the Coldstreamers continued their steady advance against last-ditch enemy stands. The 1st Battalion had stiff fighting before reaching Maubeuge, but on 10th November the Guards were on the banks of the Sambre and on the following day, at 11.00 a.m., the Armistice took effect. A week later the Guards set off for the Rhine, and within a month were stationed around Cologne. The regiment was now part of the Army of Occupation of Germany.

Following the Armistice, the Guards Division spent two months at Cologne, and the only wartime formation of the Coldstream Guards – the 4th (Pioneer) Battalion – was disbanded on 18 February 1919. In England the regiment returned to peacetime duties.

World War II

Between 1919 and 1939 the three battalions all had their stint of service abroad. The 3rd served at Constantinople in 1922–3 as part of the Army of the Black Sea. The 2nd Battalion was in the Shanghai Defence Force – first Coldstreamers to be stationed in this area – from 1927 to 1928. Then the 1st Battalion was in Egypt and the Sudan in 1932–3. The 3rd Battalion was in Palestine for a spell in 1937, but almost immediately after its return to England it went back again to the Middle East.

Although Army cutting-back had been merciless in the mid-thirties, by 1938 it had become obvious that a modern Army was absolutely necessary, and to that end, among other things, battalion transport was motorized. On 3 September 1939 when World War II broke out, the regiment was as ready as ever to take its place in the line.

Both 1st and 2nd Battalions quickly moved to France and by October were on the borders of Belgium, not far from Lille. When the German invasion burst upon the Low Countries in May 1940, the two battalions were involved at once, the 1st fighting on the north-western outskirts of Leuven along the River Dyle. Falling back in accordance with orders, the Coldstreamers repulsed the most determined enemy attacks, but soon they retired back to the French frontier. From this point onwards it was a matter of battling to maintain the shrinking perimeter of the Dunkirk pocket. Everywhere the refugee streams poured along the roads, immobilizing troops and transport, under the attacks of the ever-present dive-bombers. The 1st Battalion was able to get away from Dunkirk after a sharp fight north of Veurne and was reunited with the 2nd, one of the last units to leave the beaches, in England at the beginning of June. In the few weeks of fighting the two battalions had suffered 444 officers and men killed or wounded.

The 3rd Battalion had been in Egypt since 1937. In 1940 it was in the Western Desert as a partially motorized battalion, where it was engaged in frontier patrol duties as part of the 7th Armoured Division. It fought brilliantly when the Italian Army made its advance in September of that year and then took part in Wavell's great desert offensive. Then it joined the 2nd Scots Guards in the Nile Delta to form the 22nd Guards Brigade.

After intensive training the brigade was on the Libyan border in April 1941, coming face to face with Rommel's Afrika Korps, which was pressing

Drum major, present-day dress. The Band of the Coldstream Guards at the Duke of York's Headquarters, Chelsea (Crown copyright)

30

eastwards. During April and May the 3rd Battalion was continually in action against the Germans, and for eleven days held the important Halfaya Pass until ordered to withdraw. Subsequently the brigade was completely motorized and settled down to further training in the rear areas.

In Auchinleck's November offensive the 3rd Battalion was quickly off the mark, forming part of a mobile column sent directly across the desert to Ajdābiyah to cut off the enemy retreating from Benghazi. In January 1942 the Afrika Korps attacked with very strong armoured forces, and there was no alternative but to withdraw to Gazala, forty miles west of Tobruk.

In May 1942 Rommel was again on the offensive, battering remorselessly at the British defences. The 3rd Battalion was now in the famous 'Knightsbridge Box', a defensive area fifty miles south-west of Tobruk, and for seventeen days resisted everything the Germans could throw at them. Every day saw the enemy tanks driving recklessly up to the Coldstreamers' lines, pounding them with shells while enemy long-range guns also joined in. The Coldstreamers stuck it out but, when both adjoining positions had been abandoned or overrun, they were ordered to retire. The battalion moved back into Tobruk itself and was there when the fortress surrendered. But as no orders had been received and complete confusion prevailed, several companies of the battalion decided against submitting to the surrender, manned their trucks and drove off at speed through the encircling Germans, finally joining the main British Army many miles to the east.

In October the now re-styled 201 Guards Brigade moved to Syria for rest and training and to await replacements from home.

The 2nd Battalion landed at Algiers in November 1942 as a part of the Anglo-American invasion force, and immediately moved off towards Tunisia where a fierce battle was in progress. The Germans were reacting strongly to the pressure from the west, and an Allied attempt to seize Tunis was unsuccessful. The Coldstreamers lost heavily in the fighting for a topographical feature named 'Longstop Hill'. There followed a period of army reserve, involving rapid switches from one part of the front to another as successive attacks were mounted; the Germans' aim was to force back the

1st Army before the 8th could intervene from the east. In April 1943 the Coldstreamers became part of the 6th Armoured Division which made a dramatic thrust through the Fondouk Pass to link up with the 8th Army. Slowly but surely the pincers were closing upon Tunis, and Allied troops were soon only a few miles distant.

Meantime the 3rd Battalion had rejoined the 8th Army from Syria and on 6 March 1943 it was hotly engaged with the German forces at Médenine. The advance rolled on, and in the assault on the Mareth Line the Coldstreamers had to attack a series of low hills – the 'Horseshoe feature' as it was called – which were strongly defended by extensive mine-fields backed up by machine-gun posts. It was finally taken at the cost of heavy casualties, but despite these losses the battalion was in action again at Enfidaville at the end of April. By now both the 2nd and 3rd Battalions were splendidly reunited in the 6th Armoured Division, and took an active part in the final assault on Tunis. When the city had been occupied both battalions swept south to encircle the German garrison of Enfidaville, but the enemy made a general surrender on the 12th, and the desert war was over.

The 3rd Battalion took part in the Salerno landing on the west coast of Italy on 9th September. The success of this enterprise was for some time in doubt, and for nine days, until the Germans gave way before the threat of the arrival of the 8th Army from the south, the situation was fraught with the possibility of failure.

From this time onwards the battalion was hardly ever out of action, fighting its way northwards through hilly country across the River Volturno, up to the Garigliano, and to the mountain known as Monte Camino. Before this position was taken, two very bitter battles had to be fought against the most determined opposition, and success hung in the balance until 11th December. After this victory and a short period of rest the 3rd Battalion was engaged in the crossing of the Garigliano at the end of January 1944, and then a lengthy period of hammering at the enemy, whose defensive tactics were splendid and who took a heavy toll of the Coldstreamers. After more than their share of fighting they were relieved for a time, but in April the battalion was part of the

24th Guards Brigade right in the heart of the Apennine Mountains at Rionera. After the fall of Cassino, the Allied advance gained a degree of momentum and on 6th June the battalion passed through Rome. But from there on the advance slowed down, and heavy casualties were suffered during the fighting at Florence on the River Arno. After a month of rest and regrouping the battalion was again on the Arno at the end of August and some time later found itself in the mountains through which passed the road from Florence to Bologna. Bad weather hampered operations and

1st Battalion Coldstream Guards in Norway, March 1969. A section pauses for observation during an advance to forward positions in the mountains (Crown copyright)

the passes were strongly defended. Preparations were made to mount a major attack, but it was cancelled by extremely bad weather, and the battalion was withdrawn from the line for the last time on 16 February 1945. They sailed for home on 1st April.

The 2nd Battalion landed at Naples on 5 February 1944, part of the 1st Guards Brigade. It was immediately sent into action beyond the Garigliano, where a most bitter battle was in progress in the mountains. For twelve days the fighting went on in appalling conditions of cold and rain, with heavy losses being suffered against a dogged German resistance. In April the battalion was in the ruins of Cassino, by this time a mere collection of heaps of rubble. In April and again in May the battalion held the line at Cassino, until on 17th May the Germans withdrew. By 18th June they had reached Perugia, and there was heavy and

prolonged fighting at Monte Pacciano, but by the end of August the Coldstreamers had fought their way up to the Gothic line. The enemy had withdrawn beyond it in many places, however, and the 2nd Battalion pushed on through the mountains between Forli and Bologna. After a very welcome period of rest in Florence, efforts were made to maintain the general advance, but the country was under several feet of snow.

In February 1945 the battalion was withdrawn for reorganization, but by 1st March it was again in the field, fighting at Lake Commachio, forcing a way through the Argenta Gap into the Po Valley. The battalion crossed this famous river on 26th April and reached the vicinity of Venice by 29th April. On 2nd May the surrender of the German forces in Italy brought hostilities to an end, with the Coldstreamers at Gorizia, some thirty miles beyond Trieste.

The 1st Battalion, re-formed after the débâcle of Dunkirk, underwent a very long period of waiting, but was finally converted to an armoured battalion and incorporated into the Guards Armoured Division. In 1941 the 5th Battalion Coldstream Guards was formed and included in the divisional infantry component. In 1943 the 1st (Armoured) Battalion was equipped with Sherman tanks, and soon after D-Day (6th June) the whole Guards Armoured Division was in Normandy. During the hard weeks of the beachhead fighting the 1st and 5th Battalions were heavily engaged. Slowly at first, but then with a rush, they gained ground. By the middle of August the 'Falaise pocket' was sealed, and there began the dash across northern France. The 1st and 5th Battalions now fought as a mutually supporting group, and together they entered Brussels on 3rd September. After the long pursuit, fighting became harder as German resistance stiffened, but nevertheless the Albert Canal was forced and the Coldstream group mounted an attack on Bourg Leopold. The enemy's defence was too strong for only two battalions, and the 5th suffered especially heavily. Next came the Arnhem operation, with the Guards Armoured Division driving north in an unsuccessful attempt to contact the airborne forces. This was followed by intensive fighting for the 'island', the area between Nijmegen and Arnhem.

In November the Coldstreamers were on

German soil just north of Maastricht, and much of the winter was spent in training, sometimes in deep snow. On 5th March the 5th Battalion, supported by the 1st, attacked a German bridgehead which controlled the Wesel crossing of the Rhine, and at the cost of many casualties broke into the defences. That night the enemy evacuated the position and withdrew across the Rhine, leaving the left bank clear. Soon tanks of the Guards Armoured Division were roaring into the very heart of Germany, heading for Bremen. On 3 April 1945 the River Emms was reached, and here Captain Lidell of the 5th Battalion won the Victoria Cross for his share in the capture of a bridge over the river. The Coldstreamers were now facing some of the best troops in the German Army – mainly parachute troops – and these did not give way readily. Every foot of ground had to be fought for with the greatest courage and determination. But nothing could interfere with the momentum of the Allied advance. At the beginning of May the 1st and 5th Battalions entered Stade on the Elbe estuary. On 5th May the German Army surrendered, and the Guards Armoured Division took possession of the great naval base at Cuxhaven.

Lastly there has to be told the story of the 4th Coldstream Guards (Tank) Battalion formed in 1940, first as an infantry unit, next motorized, then re-formed as one of the regiments of the 6th Guards Tank Brigade and equipped with Churchill tanks. The battalion, after its years of training and waiting, landed in France at the end of July 1944 and within a few days played a vital role in the break-out from Caumont. Fighting raged for two weeks in the difficult Normandy countryside, when tank stalked tank to pound each other at point-blank range. In this fighting the heavily armoured Churchills excelled, but when the pursuit across France began, it was decided to leave them in the rear for they were not fast enough. The battalion remained on the Seine until September, when it moved up to the forward areas.

Throughout October the battalion was continually fighting in Holland, first in the Overloon-Venraij district, west of the Meuse, then at Tilburg, which was occupied on 27th October. A period of training was interrupted by a call to assist in repelling the German offensive in the Ardennes, and it was then transferred to Maastricht. In mid-January 1945 it was engaged in clearing the enemy from strong positions on the left bank of the River Roer. During the following month the battalion was engaged in Operation 'Veritable', the clearing of the enemy from the area between the Meuse and the Rhine. The Churchill tanks were not used in the initial Rhine crossing, but three days later they drove forward through many well-defended positions to arrive at Munster on 2nd April; then on the Celle and northwards to Velzen. The town was occupied on 18th April, and the lower Elbe reached shortly after. Next was the city of Hamburg, which surrendered on 3rd May. On 8 May 1945 (VE day) the tanks of the Coldstreamers rumbled into Kiel, headquarters of the German Navy. It was the end of the war.

The Plates

A1 Musketeer, 1678

At this time the infantry arm was composed of two types of soldier – the pikeman and, as seen here, the musketeer. He is armed with a matchlock musket, 4 ft. in length, a short sword, and often carried a wooden fork rest on which to place the heavy musket while recharging it. The long uniform coat is of red cloth, with a white collar and sash, fastened at the front by a single row of buttons and has a buttoned-down pocket flap on each hip. The back skirt is split to the waist and also buttoned in a single row. Breeches and stockings are of the same colour as the coat, while the

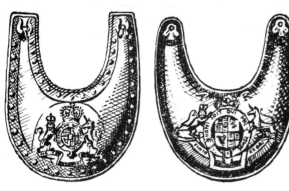

Officers' gorgets – William III and Queen Anne patterns.

The gorget was the last remaining piece of medieval armour to be worn by officers, and indicated the bearer's rank and that he was on duty. Captains of foot regiments would wear a gold gorget, lieutenants one of black studded with gold, and an ensign's gorget would have been black studded with silver

cuffs, coat lining, garters and shoestrings are green. From the musketeer's left shoulder hangs his bandoleer of cartridges – the 'twelve apostles' as it was known. This effectively prevented his moving without an accompanying rattle, thus inhibiting night manœuvres in secrecy. As well as the twelve cases, each holding one charge of powder, there hangs from the bandoleer a priming horn or flask of fine priming powder, and a bag for musket balls and a spare match. This 'match' was a piece of cord, usually dipped in vinegar or lees wine to encourage it to burn more fiercely.

A2 Pikeman, 1668
Complementing the musketeer in an infantry regiment was the pikeman, but with increasingly effective and efficient fire-power he was soon to disappear from the army. A pikeman in the Coldstreams was clothed almost totally in green, his full coat having red lining and cuffs only, and the worsted stockings bearing red garters. The coat buttoned at the front with a single row of pewter buttons, as did the split at the back of the skirt. There were two pocket flaps, one on each hip, and these were fastened down with four buttons. A steel corselet (back- and breastplates), and combe-cap (a lined steel helmet) were worn, these being more often than not blackened to preserve them and to prevent the reflection from bright steel giving away a position unnecessarily. Gen. Monck is reported to have said that his pikemen even made a practice of using the backplate as a dripping pan in which to cook. Accoutrements

included a buff belt and sword 'frog', from which hung the broadsword, a white fringed sash and the 18 ft. pike. This pike was less unwieldy than might be thought from first sight of its length, and the fifteen complicated drill orders for pikemen from the *New Modle* army drill book of the time, and it could, indeed, be shorter depending upon the taste of its owner.

A3 Drum Major, 1670
Much less elaborately costumed than later successors, the drum major of this period is rather plainly clad in red coat and stockings, his cuffs and coat lining being green, as are the shoestrings. A crimson sash hangs from his right shoulder, on which is also a decoration of green cords. The staff is of brown or black Malacca cane and has a silver knob.

B1 Grenadier, 1684
This figure shows the original 'grenadier' – the big, powerful man selected to throw the first primitive grenade, and from whom the later grenadier – the *élite* soldier – developed. The head-dress is made from the old red stocking, or fatigue cap, and in the case of the Coldstreams this cap had a green cloth front and back added to it, edged with wide yellow lace, and bearing the royal Cypher of Charles II and the fleurs-de-lis on the front. This head-dress was originally designed for the purpose of allowing freedom of movement when throwing the grenade with an overarm action, and, later, when slinging the musket over the shoulder – the grenadiers being the only company to have a sling on their firearms at this time. The broad-brimmed tricorne would have been readily dislodged by this action. The full red coat is worn buttoned up the front with pewter buttons and yellow-laced buttonholes. The yellow lace and green cuffs are still distinctive of the regiment, although this colour would be changed to blue before long. A broad buff crossbelt was worn, with a large leather pouch for carrying grenades and matches. The belt about the waist had a 'frog' fastening to hold the short sword and plug-bayonet.

B2 Private, 1742
The uniform shown is that recorded in the first official regulations, the *Representation of the Cloathing*

of His Majesty's Household, published in accordance with an order of George II. The head-dress is as worn by the centre companies of the Coldstream Guards, consisting of a black felt tricorne hat, turned up at both sides and at the back, the brim of which is edged with white lace. On the side over the left eye appears a black silk Hanover cockade, bearing a gold loop over a regimental button. The red coat has blue lapels edged with white lace, the buttons and buttonhole lace being arranged in pairs. The lapels and skirt are buttoned back, probably to save any hindrance when marching, and reveal the red waistcoat and blue coat lining. The blue breeches are of the colour worn by the Foot Guards and all 'Royal' line regiments, and long white spatterdashes (or gaiters) cover black shoes. Equipment carried at this time included a bayonet suspended over the left hip from a 'frog' attached to the waist-belt, a hanger (or short cutlass), a cartouche (or ammunition bag) and the flintlock Tower musket known as the 'Brown Bess'.

B3 Grenadier, 1747
A change has occurred since 1742, the waist-belt now being worn over the waistcoat and under the unbuttoned coat. The 'mitre cap' is similar to that of the grenadiers of all three regiments of Foot Guards, and the White Horse of Hanover appears on the front flap. The grenadier carries a basket-hilted sword, and while gaiters were generally worn – white for dress occasions and grey or black otherwise – occasionally it seems that stockings were worn by themselves. Over the left shoulder is a buff crossbelt, which still bears the match case – a relic of the days of the matchlock musket, the flintlock 'Brown Bess' now being carried in its place. Suspended from the crossbelt at the right hip is the cartouche or ammunition bag.

C1 Private, Grenadier Company (full dress), 1760
The red cloth coat is that worn by all privates and is long, loose fitting and with blue lapels, these latter extending well below the waistline, turned back and fastened by ten pewter buttons. These buttons, arranged in pairs, are edged with white tape and white buttonhole lace. The skirt is also turned back, lined white and held by a small worsted grenade where each side joins. The back of

the skirt has ornamental pocket flaps, decorated with white lace and four pewter buttons, again spaced in pairs. The grenadier is distinguished by the projecting winged epaulettes of flank companies which are blue, and decorated with six small white lace loops in pairs. The waistcoat, buckskin breeches and full-dress spatterdashes (a type of long gaiter) are all white. For service dress black spatterdashes would be worn. The head-dress of this period is a bearskin cap, shaped as a mitre with the fur brushed upwards. The back of the cap is of red cloth with a grenade embroidered in the centre, while at the front is a copper plate, black japanned and embossed in white metal. On the crest is a scroll bearing the Hanover motto: *Nec Aspera Terrent*. The kit carried by a grenadier consisted of a white buff waist-belt, on the left side of which was a 'frog' fastening that held the bayonet and hanger. This belt was worn over the waistcoat but beneath the coat. Attached to the back of the buff crossbelt was a large black cartouche box decorated with the Royal Cypher in brass. The short Land pattern musket of 1750 is carried, with a socket-bayonet and short cutlass or hanger.

C2 Sergeant (half dress), 1789
The sergeant, who belongs to one of the battalion companies, carries the traditional halberd of the 1700–92 pattern. In 1792 sergeants ceased to carry the halberd, and it was replaced by a half-pike or spontoon. He also carries his cane, suspended by a cord from a button high on the left lapel. The hat is plain, but ornamented with looping and a white feather, and rank is indicated by the single fringed epaulette worn on the right shoulder. The lace and buttons are now arranged in pairs – indicating the wearer belongs to the 2nd Regiment of Foot Guards. White breeches and waistcoat together with short black gaiters are worn, and the crimson sergeant's waist sash is beneath the coat and knotted on the left hip.

C3 Drummer (service dress), 1790
This figure shows the beginning of the characteristic drummer's uniform, with great similarities to that of the present day. The head-dress is a black bearskin cap, with the fur brushed upwards concealing a red cloth crown, and bears a black metal

plate with the Royal Cypher and regimental title in white metal thereupon. A red-and-white plume is on the left side of the bearskin – the plume being red at its base – with white cap lines attached. The red coat is almost entirely ornamented with white regimental drummer's lace – the Guards' pattern for this lace being made of white worsted upon which are worked blue fleurs-de-lis. The blue collar and flank company winged epaulettes are fringed in plain white and blue, and the cuffs and lapels edged with plain white lace. Upon the lapels are five pairs of buttons and white-laced buttonholes. The turnbacks to the coat are false and made from white cloth, again edged with drummer's lace. There are two buttons at the back waist seams, and a pocket flap on each hip decorated with lace and two pairs of buttons and laced buttonholes. Lace also ornaments the back and sleeve seams. The waistcoat and breeches are white, and in full dress white spatterdashes with black straps beneath each knee would be worn. The drummer in service dress shown here wears black gaiters. A drummer's kit was, necessarily, centred around his instrument. The drum is blue-fronted and bears the Royal Arms and Garter Star; the hoops are white, edged with red and have a central wavy blue line. One regimental peculiarity is that the drum sling is of the fleurs-de-lis pattern. The crossbelts have a 'frog' fastening on the left hip for the drummer's sword or hanger, and also attached is his fife case. The hilt of the hanger was brass, and had a curved blade 27½ in. long contained in a black leather scabbard with two brass mounts.

D1 Officer (half dress), 1790

The scarlet coat has a stand-up collar – the coat collars of other ranks at this time being of the turned-down type, although worn fastened up – and the cuffs, collar and long lapels are laced with gold. Buttons are spaced in pairs, as are the gilt lace loops, and a gilt gorget – indicating that the wearer is on duty – is held in place by blue ribbons and rosettes. Knee-length black boots are worn with half dress, while full dress would include the thigh-length, white spatterdashes. The crimson waist sash is knotted under the coat on the left side, while the sword is suspended from a white crossbelt. No hat feather was worn at this time.

D2 Grenadier (half dress), 1808

The uniform is that of a grenadier at the height of the Napoleonic Wars. The front of the short jacket is ornamented with buttons and lace arranged in pairs. The blue-winged epaulettes of the flank companies are laced with white, and the bearskin is ornamented with white cap lines, a white plume and bears a small brass plate in the front. The bearskin itself was not issued to the whole regiment until considerably later, the battalion companies wearing the standard shako of the period. A brass plate is placed at the junction of the white buff crossbelts, and the musket is the celebrated 'Brown Bess'.

D3 Colour Sergeant, Grenadier Company (half dress), 1815

In this figure the elaborate badge, peculiar to the Guards and denoting the wearer's rank or function, is seen on the upper right arm, but was worn on both. It consists of three gold lace chevrons bearing the King's Colour with crossed swords beneath and surmounted by a crown. Indicative of the company to which he belongs, the colour sergeant wears a small silver grenade on each epaulette. The red coat is single-breasted, fastens in front with five pairs of regimental brass buttons decorated with gold lace, and has the skirts turned back to reveal white lining. There are two buttons at the back waist seams, and also two pocket flaps edged with gold lace in four panels, each panel having a brass button in the centre. A crimson sash is worn around the waist, knotted on the left hip with two tassels hanging down at the side. In half and full dress the 12-in.-high bearskin cap bearing the Royal Arms and regimental title on a brass plate is worn, while on service this would be replaced by the Wellington shako with a white plume. Full dress would also include the thigh-length white spatterdashes in place of half-dress gaiters, while on active service yet another difference appearing by this time would have been charcoal-grey trousers over black gaiters. Weapons included – for Foot Guards and senior N.C.O.s – the sword of the 1803 pattern, with brass hilt and fishskin grip bound by twisted silver wire, and having a slightly curved blade encased in a black leather scabbard with two brass mounts. The topmost of these mounts bore a stud which fitted into the 'frog' on the crossbelt. The most distinctive weapon is the infantry sergeant's pike – regulation issue from 1792 to 1830 – known from 1803 as the spontoon.

E1 Drum Major (service dress), 1815

Like all drum majors that of the Coldstream Guards wore a richly ornamented uniform. The scarlet coatee has a blue collar and cuffs, all edged with gold lace. The front of the coatee is single-breasted, has three rows of brass buttons, arranged in pairs, and gold lace bars and button-holes stretching the width of the chest. The sleeves are decorated with rows of regimental gold lace, and this lace also extends down the outer side seams. There are two buttons at the back waist seams and two pocket slashes decorated with four panels of gold lace, arranged in pairs with a button in the centre of each. Gold lace also orna-ments all the back seams. In 1812 the Wellington or Belgic shako was introduced as a head-dress, and this, too, is very elaborately ornamented. Made from black felt, it has an 8½-in.-high false front and bears a brass plate in the shape of a shield surmounted by a crown with the Garter Star in the centre. On service the drum major wears, as seen here, black gaiters; in full dress these would be replaced by long white spatter-dashes reaching almost to the thigh, with buff straps below each knee. Over the right shoulder is a white crossbelt, in the centre of which is an oval plate of brass bearing a Garter Star, and on the left hip a 'frog' for the sword. Over the left shoulder is the drum major's blue *baldric*, edged with gold lace and bearing the Royal Cypher, Garter Star and two small drumsticks. Indicative of all drum majors is the mace, mounted with gold and wrapped with gold cords and tassels. In State dress the drum major would wear a uniform hat and coat very similar to that worn today, the only differences being white breeches instead of blue, and a buff crossbelt with a sword.

E2 Officer, Flank Company (cloaked), 1815

The greatcoat with cape introduced during the Napoleonic Wars is worn over the officer's service-dress uniform. Previous to this period there was no similar garment.

E3 Officer, Grenadier Company (half dress), 1815

This officer, in service or half dress, wears a double-breasted scarlet coatee of the 1812 pattern, with two rows of ten gilt buttons arranged in pairs. The coat is buttoned over so that the facings and lace are almost concealed, with the exception of the blue lapel facings, but the collar is left open to show a white shirt frill, below which is worn a small gold gorget. This latter was indicative of the officer's status and derived from the last article of medieval armour to be utilized. Its presence usually indicated that the bearer was on duty. At the back of the coatee there would appear two buttons at the waist seams, and two pocket flaps edged with gold lace, bearing four buttons spaced in pairs. A characteristic of all flank companies were the winged epaulettes. Those worn by the grenadier company were liberally laced in gold and bore a small grenade worked in gold wire. Around the waist is a crimson net sash, knotted on the left hip, with four tassels. When opened out, these tassels would appear at each corner, and the sash was often used to carry wounded officers from the field of battle as well as for pure decoration. In full dress this officer would wear white breeches and long white spatterdashes, buttoned on the outer side of each leg, extending to the thigh with a blue garter and gilt buckle worn below the knees. In half dress either black gaiters would be worn or, as shown here, black hessian boots with gold tassels at the front.

F1 Colour Sergeant (full dress), 1831

The figure shown is in the full dress of the period – a period notable for the increasing elaboration of military uniform. The tall bearskin cap is 21 in. high, swelling out at the top, and has a crown and rose badge at the front. A small leather peak is almost totally covered by long fur. The scarlet cut feather plume has two large gold tassels, and the

Regimental button, 1820. Prior to this date the Garter Star motto was replaced by the words 'Coldstream Guards'

curb chain is of interlocking brass rings on a black leather backing. The double-breasted coat is scarlet (not the normal other ranks' medder red) and is embroidered in gold. Gold lace panels appear on the blue cuffs, back pocket slashes and skirt turnbacks. These latter are white cloth and fixed at the bottom with a Garter Star. The collar is 3 in. high and has a gold lace gorget embroidered on each side. Epaulettes are also of gold lace with heavy fringe, and bear a brass crescent and silver wire rose on top. On each arm is the distinctive rank badge – three gold lace chevrons, decorated with the King's Colour and crossed swords, and surmounted by a gold crown. The waist sash is crimson, the knots falling at the left hip, and the trousers are of a 'dark mixture' without the red stripe. The colour sergeant carries a sergeant's carbine – a smaller version of the India pattern musket – with a 37-in. barrel and 0·65-in. bore. A socket-bayonet was used at this time, and the sword is that of the Foot Guard 1816 regimental pattern with a brass hilt, black grips and a black leather scabbard with two brass mounts. The equipment consists of two white buff crossbelts – one supporting the black leather cartouche bearing a brass Garter Star, and the other over the right shoulder holding the 'frog' fastening for sword and bayonet. On the left hip would be a white canvas haversack, while a wooden water-bottle can be seen on the right. A black valise upon which is painted a white Garter Star is worn on the back, supported by two buff shoulder-straps with a third strap passing across the chest under the crossbelts. Rolled on top of this valise is the greatcoat, attached to which is a mess tin. When the greatcoat was being worn, the mess tin, in a black cover, was fixed to the top of the valise.

F2 Private (service dress), 1831

The private's uniform was much the same as that of the pioneer of the same period. He wears the ordinary ranks' double-breasted red coatee, with blue cuffs and high Prussian collar ornamented with plain white worsted lace. The epaulettes are white cloth with heavy white worsted fringe, and the coat buttons are pewter. The only difference between the coats of pioneer and private is the omission of the badge, bearing the crossed axes,

from the arms of the latter. In service, or winter dress, the private wears blue trousers with a 2-in. red stripe. The knapsack bears the Garter Star in white, and the long, 1780 India pattern musket and socket-bayonet are used. The crossbelt which, unlike that of the pioneer, has a brass star in the centre, is fitted with a small chain with a brush at its end, its purpose being to clean the touch-hole of the musket which rapidly fouled when fired several times. Neither a sword nor a sash were worn.

F3 Officer (summer dress), 1831

This officer wears the typical tall bearskin cap, 21 in. high, swelling out at the top and bearing a gilt rose and crown badge on the front. On the right side is a scarlet cut feather plume, 12 in. long, with two gold bullion tassels. The curb chain is of gilt interlocking rings, backed with black leather and lined with velvet. The double-breasted scarlet coatee has a 3-in.-high Prussian collar, fastened at the front, and a gold bullion gorget patch bearing a Garter Star embroidered on each side. The coatee buttons are gilt and have the pattern of the Garter Star upon them. Two gold lace epaulettes are worn, with bullion fringe and a burnished gilt crescent and silver wire rose embroidered on the top of each. The cuffs are blue and have four gold wire panels extending upwards with a gilt button in each panel. The skirts are lined white with false turnbacks, at the join of which is a gold embroidered Garter Star. At the back waist seam are two gilt buttons, and two pocket flaps also ornamented with gilt buttons and gold bars. Between 1st May and 14th October white, summer-dress trousers were worn, winter dress having blue trousers with a 2-in. scarlet stripe. The State sash is crimson and gold and worn about the waist with the tassels falling at the left hip. A white buff crossbelt bears a gilt rectangular plate with a silver Garter Star in the centre, and attached to the belt is a 'frog' from which hangs the 1833 pattern sword for infantry officers. This sword had a gilt half-basket hilt with the Royal Cypher inserted between the bars, a black fishskin grip bound with gilt wire, and a buff sword knot. For State dress this knot would be gold. A 32½-in., slightly curved blade was contained in a black leather scabbard with three gilt